Miss Fane
—IN INDIA—

Miss Fane
—IN INDIA—

EDITED BY
JOHN PEMBLE

ALAN
SUTTON
1985

Alan Sutton Publishing Limited
Brunswick Road · Gloucester

First published 1985

British Library Cataloguing in Publication Data

Fane, Isabella
Miss Fane in India.
1. British—India—History—19th century
2. India—Social life and customs
I. Title   II. Pemble, John
954.03'14   DS428

ISBN 0-86299-240-0

Jacket picture
Courtesy of The Fine Art Society, London

Typesetting and origination by
Alan Sutton Publishing Limited
Printed in Great Britain

CONTENTS

ACKNOWLEDGEMENTS

I wish to offer my best thanks to Mrs H.W.N. Fane, owner of the Fane papers deposited in the Lincolnshire Records Office, for her kind permission to print the journal and letters of Isabella Fane. I am especially grateful for having had the opportunity of discussing the project with her and the late Captain Fane at Fulbeck Hall.

It was Professor Jack Simmons who first drew my attention to the Fane papers at Lincoln. I am very glad to record my deep sense of gratitude to him – both for this, and for a multitude of other services and kindnesses.

Mr C.M. Lloyd, the Lincolnshire County Archivist, and Miss Mary Finch, the Deputy Archivist, gave me invaluable assistance. Miss Finch's wide knowledge led me to the portrait of Isabella that is reproduced in this volume. It is a pleasure to acknowledge my debt to its owner, for her ready response to my inquiries and her generous permission to have the portrait photographed and published. All the illustrations in the book were copied by the Photographic Unit of the Faculty of Arts in the University of Bristol, and the map is reproduced from C.C. Davies, *Historical Atlas of the Indian Peninsula*, by permission of Oxford University Press.

J. P.

INTRODUCTION

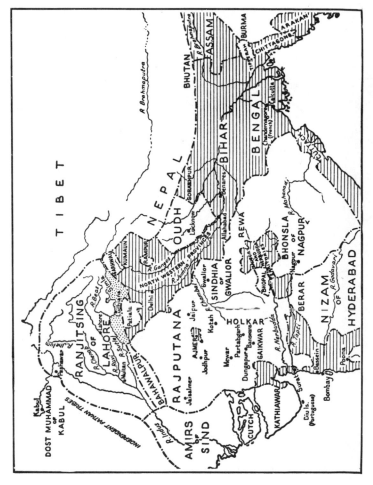

Northern India in 1836.
Areas under British rule and protection are shaded.

INTRODUCTION

1. *Miss Fane and her Contemporaries*

English ladies of the nineteenth century were used to leisure; nevertheless leisure was a problem in India, where the climate frequently made even gentle pastimes exhausting. In the hot weather winding silk, cutting paper and tatting seemed like labours of Hercules. 'Nearly unmitigated *ennui* is the lot of the majority of luckless women', sighed Emma Roberts, recalling life in India in the 1830s. 'During the greater part of the year the slightest exertion is toil . . . The punkah,* also, is very inimical to occupation; there is no possibility of enduring existence out of the reach of this enormous fan, and while it is waving to and fro weights are requisite to secure every article upon the table. Should they be unadvisedly removed, away flies the whole apparatus to different parts of the room.' Even 'tending flowers, the truly feminine employment' was out of the question. 'The garden may be full of plants, in all the abundance and beauty of native luxuriance, but, except before the sun has risen, or after it has set, they are not to be approached; and even then the frame is too completely enervated by the climate to admit of those pleasing little labours which render the greenhouse and the parterre so interesting.'[1]

---

* Before the days of the electrical revolving fan, 'punkah' (Hindi *pankha*) referred to a batten-type, swinging ceiling fan, operated, through a series of cords and pulleys, by a 'punkah-wallah' – a native servant who squatted in a corner of the room or outside the door and whose sole function was to keep the contraption moving.

3

Their loss is our gain, because one thing that was still possible was writing. Many ladies turned to this in their predicament and they have left, in their journals and letters, one of our richest sources of information about British life in India. They were better attuned to domestic detail and social incident than their menfolk, whose literary remains are legion but whose preoccupations tended to be tiger hunts, military exploits and politics. Some of these ladies wrote with considerable skill. Mrs Sherwood's descriptions of life in Indian military cantonments, where 'a hollow, church-like sound' ran along empty halls and galleries; and her pictures of British households, with their cohorts of swarthy servants, tantrums of spoilt children, creaking punkahs and sickly smell of rosewater, are as evocative as anything in Kipling. Emily Eden, eldest sister of the Governor-General, Lord Auckland (1836–42), has left us albums of sharp verbal snapshots of life in the highest official circles, as well as confession of preference for dusky males that carries distinctly Forsterian suggestions of suppressed libido awakening to India's erotic summons. 'An infantry review is rather a dull sight', she wrote; 'but this was striking, for the sepoys [native infantrymen] seem to me to be much finer soldiers than our people, partly from being so tall and upright; and then I am convinced that brown is the natural colour for man – black and white are unnatural deviations, and look shocking. I am quite ashamed of our white skins.'[2] Other ladies, like Mrs Meer Hassan Ali (the English wife of a Muslim scholar) and Mrs Fanny Parks, learnt the native languages and recorded valuable information about Indian life and manners. Their work is now largely forgotten; but it well deserves to be taken down, dusted and looked at again. It makes intriguing reading – not only as the record of a lost experience, but as a corrective to the notion that all Englishwomen in India were of the straitlaced *memsahib*

Miss Fane and her Contemporaries

type – snobbish, imperious and racially prejudiced; intruders who destroyed the harmonious relationship between British men and native society.

Isabella Fane was a member of this literary sisterhood. Born in 1804, she was General Sir Henry Fane's only daughter, and the second of his four children. Her mother was Isabella Cooke (née Gorges), of Dublin, who was Sir Henry's consort for many years and who later styled herself Lady Fane, but whom he never in fact married, owing to legal impediments in the way of a dissolution of her first marriage. Isabella accompanied her father to India on his appointment as Commander-in-Chief in 1835, and acted as his hostess until the end of 1838, when, in anticipation of military operations beyond the northwest frontier, she was sent back to the family home at Fulbeck, in Lincolnshire. During most of her time in India she sent monthly letters home, addressed not to her mother, with whom she was never on good terms, but to her paternal aunt, Mrs Caroline Chaplin of Blankney, in Lincolnshire; and it is from these that the greater part of the text which follows is taken. The surviving letters form a sequence with one interruption, but those relating to the outward journey and first three months in India are lost. The sequence comes to an end in April 1837. There is, however, a separate record of her years in India in a journal, and this has been used to supplement the letters in the text. About two thirds of the manuscript material have been used, and the selections are printed as written, save that punctuation has been modified, the occasional solecism corrected, and spelling standardized. Where the MS offers alternative spellings of the same word, the more frequent version has been chosen and used throughout. Editorial matter, including modern transliterations of Indian names, is in square brackets and footnotes.

Isabella Fane's letters are rich in historical and human interest. They are the chronicle of a single woman in a

5

man's world, forced to come to terms with the prospect of a lonely and rootless future as her years increase and the chances of marriage elude her one by one; and at the same time they are a lively record of the private lives of the *sahibs* and *memsahibs* of the early days of the Raj. Isabella moved in the highest circles, and plied her aunt with gossip and anecdote of the sort that Jane Austen would have relished, but which seldom got into print. Hers is a rare picture of that vanished world, because it was never adjusted for publication. In one place she does talk about publication; but nothing ever came of it, and it would have been a pity if anything had, because the whole flavour of the letters must have changed in the process. She would probably have tried to embellish them with appropriate 'bursts of good writing interspersed with sensible remarks', such as she admired in Mrs Buller's Journal; and what now seems most alluring must inevitably have fallen victim to some editorial blue pencil. No Victorian publisher would have allowed her intimate revelations about mosquito bites and boils, let alone her caustic comments on notabilities like Sir Charles Metcalfe, Mrs Prinsep, Julia Margaret Cameron, the Misses Eden and all those military grotesques. Even if ladies talked like that, they were not supposed to write like it. Miss Fane wrote as she talked, and her letters are free from the usual trappings of Victorian travel memoirs – stilted description, sententious moralizing and hidebound discretion. They are not polished, and they are not deep; but they are loud and clear – even a little shrill – amid a welter of muffled voices. From them we learn a lot that others would never have allowed us to know; and we know Miss Fane as she really was – derisive, indignant, ironic, and more than a little vulnerable behind her uncouth sense of fun.

There is not much glamour about Isabella's Raj. In fact, if there is one thing that her letters leave no doubt about, it is the acute discomfort of life in India. This comes across as the most harrowing aspect of experience there – more harrowing even than the repeated appearance of Death's head at the imperial banquet. Isabella can confront death with comparative equanimity – not because she is callous, but because she assumes that death is controllable, whereas lesser calamities are not. Early nineteenth-century medicine may not be convincing now; but it was convincing in its day, and it fulfilled medicine's traditional purpose, in that it gave death and disease the logicality of retribution. An effect of its rituals and precepts was to make death's visitations seem less random and indiscriminate: less the result of misfortune than of disobedience – or 'folly' as Isabella would say. But neither wealth nor science could claim the power to avert discomfort. Things like insects, dust, smells, heat, cold, glare, immense distances and interminable receptions defied armies of servants and batteries of mechanical contrivances. They made existence a gratuitous penance of itching, sweating, swelling, sore eyes, intestinal rebellion and general exhaustion and stress.

Another interesting feature of these letters is their treatment of native society. Miss Fane in Calcutta is generally indifferent and dismissive. Her interest in things Indian does not extend beyond the picturesque and the sensational. She has few contacts with natives apart from servants, and her exchanges with these are minimal. 'We are too imperfect in the language', she writes, 'to go beyond asking for what we want; and as for understanding what they say, it is quite out of the question.' In reading her letters we are aware of the native inhabitants of the country only as remote and anonymous supernumeraries, existing in some limbo outside the natural range of human concern and sympathy. Even princes and dignitaries are not named. They feature as 'the Nepaul General', 'Rajah somebody', 'the Mahratta chief'. In the Punjab, on the other hand, her interest is awakened. She shows curiosity about the Sikh way of life and Sikh politics. Personalities are named, their characters assessed and their family relationships carefully explained. This part of her work absolves her from the charge of colour prejudice. Despite some unflattering references to the Bengalis as 'Blackees' it is clear that, as was so often the case with transient visitors, colour had less significance for her than it had for the resident British community. She happily admits her admiration for the handsome Sikh soldiers, just as her male companions admitted theirs for the Sikh women. The explanation for her responses lies elsewhere.

Her Calcutta aloofness derived partly from the colonial situation in Bengal. Social distance followed from the fact that the Bengalis were a conquered people; contempt from the fact that they were ignominiously conquered. The ease with which their resistance had been overcome at the battle of Plassey (1757) had stamped them once and for all, in British estimation, as soft and effeminate – qualities scorned by a people who prided themselves on their martial and athletic prowess. The Sikhs of the Punjab, on the other hand, were independent and warlike. In their territories the British were not masters, lording it over the native population by right of conquest, but guests with a healthy respect for the military potential of their hosts. Class-consciousness, too, no doubt played its part in determining Miss Fane's responses. In Bengal the British were a ruling élite. The natives (including the erstwhile aristocracy) were the 'lower orders', and were expected to keep their distance in much the same way as the lower orders at home. In the Punjab the Sikhs were the ruling élite, and were consequently treated on terms of equality. It is noteworthy that these responses became traditional, and survived changed military and political circumstances to determine the bias of British sympathy throughout the history of the Raj. It was always the Punjab and the northwest that got the lion's share of attention in popular English literature on India. Finally, in Bengal the aloofness of the British was enhanced by the fact that discrimination was practised against, as well as by them. The Hindu pollution-complex precluded interchanges of the type best known to upper-class English women and not unnaturally blighted the compassion and interest of even the best-intentioned. An anonymous English woman writing in the *Calcutta Review* in 1845 pinpointed this sense of rejection:

> In England, anyone whose heart awakens to a desire of usefulness has but to hold out a hand to the objects that every day presents. Here, on the contrary, we hardly know how to exert any kindness, beyond that of giving money. Our servants are ill, – they go to their own houses; we may stop at the door as we pass, in the evening or morning, and ask how they are, but our entrance would be unwelcome, and often impossible; and, if admitted, we should find no reception for the comforts we desire to administer. If we bring refreshment for the body, our touch has polluted it; if we would speak peace to the soul there is no common ground on which we can stand. These circumstances produce a deadening influence on the heart, and tend to extinguish its best desires.

2. India in the 1830s

When Miss Fane arrived in India the British were direct rulers of some 540,000 square miles of territory. This was made up chiefly of the Gangetic plain and delta in the north (the Bengal Presidency) and, joined by a narrow belt of land along the eastern coast, the appendix of the subcontinent in the south (the Madras and Bombay Presidencies). In the intervening space were the main princely states – Hyderabad, Nagpur,

9

Gwalior, Indore, Baroda – and the dozens of smaller principalities composing the area called Rajputana. These states, covering about 700,000 square miles, were mere remnants of their former selves: vestiges remaining after much of their territory and most of their independence had been mortgaged to the British. Originally, the British had come to India to trade, hoping to exchange woollens and metals for cotton, indigo and saltpetre; but they had discovered a more profitable commodity in the native battalions that they were so adept at training. During the eighteenth century India was in turmoil, and the warring native princes had bought the military services of the British with cash subsidies – only to discover, like the animals in the fable, that it is easier to invite a lion to join you than to ask him to leave. They had saved themselves from their Indian enemies at the cost of saddling themselves with troops who were more efficient than their own and who obeyed a foreign master. Economic instability often compelled the princes to commute the cash subsidies for grants of land, and so by means of this 'subsidiary system' the British had acquired both a territorial empire and a widespread political suzerainty. Most native princes retained nominal control over their domestic affairs; but each had surrendered control of his foreign policy and acted besides under the eagle eye of a British agent called a Resident, who kept his own government informed of all that went on in the princely court and called the ruler to account for mismanagement or disloyalty.

Only one of India's natural frontiers remained outside British supervision. This was the Indus river, in the northwest, separating the subcontinent from central Asia. Stretching for nearly two thousand miles from deep in the Hindu Kush mountains to the Arabian Sea, it had throughout history been regarded as the threshold of India. It seemed logical therefore that the British, who had reversed the age-old direction of conquest by starting, instead of finishing in Bengal, should complete their dominion by advancing to this traditional boundary. When Isabella was in India the lure of the Indus was doubly strong. The London government was in the grip of one of its periodic fits of nerves concerning Russian ambitions in central Asia and the feeling was growing in official circles that the British must control the Indus, and even the states of Herat and Afghanistan beyond, in order to obviate the Russian threat to India.

Two independent states lay across this strategically important river. In the south was Sind, ruled by a jealous oligarchy of Muslim Amirs who were the focus of much diplomatic activity in the 1830s. Commercial treaties extorted from them in 1832 and 1834 opened the lower Indus to British shipping, and two treaties of 1838 finally reduced them to the status of subsidiary allies, encumbered with the usual apparatus of Resident and subsidiary force. Sir Henry Fane was instrumental in extracting these concessions, which were reckoned essential for the operations of his Army of the Indus. This force had originally been collected to rescue the city of Herat from the Persian puppets of Russia; but the Persians unexpectedly abandoned the city and a reduced version of the army therefore prepared, instead, to place a British protégé on the throne of Afghanistan. Sir Henry, who was feeling his age, reckoned that this would be a minor affair that could safely be left to other hands. He consequently submitted his resignation late in 1838 and retired to Bombay to await a passage home. He died at sea in 1840, too soon to learn of the disastrous issue of the first Afghan war.

North of Sind was the Punjab, the fertile land of the five rivers. It was the homeland of the Sikhs, a reformed and unshorn sect of warrior Hindus, who had made themselves its rulers. Their chief was old Ranjit Singh of Lahore, the 'Lion of the Punjab' – tiny, illiterate and

11

astute, but now impaired of speech and health following a paralytic stroke. Throughout his long career he had held the British at arm's length, drawing a prudent lesson from the fate of princes who had invited their cooperation or aroused their resentment. A treaty of 1809 had fixed the Sutlej river as the boundary between his and the British spheres of influence, and there it had remained ever since, Ranjit taking care to direct his own ambitions and the martial energies of his followers either north into Afghanistan or south into Sind. His suspicions concerning British intentions had kept diplomatic exchanges to a minimum and few British officials had ever been invited to Lahore. By the 1830s, however, he was feeling the need of British moral support. He was at daggers drawn with one of the rulers of Afghanistan and was anxious to ensure a smooth succession for his son after his own death. These preoccupations led him to break a habit and invite top members of the British Indian government to the wedding of his grandson, Prince Nao Nihal Singh, in March 1837. The Governor-General declined, fearing lest acceptance should impair good relations with Afghanistan; but the Fanes went, and we have in Isabella's letters a description of the celebrations at Lahore which rivals, both in liveliness of style and historical interest, Emily Eden's account of the Governor-General's encounter with Ranjit Singh in November the following year.

3. *The British Raj*

The invasion of Afghanistan in 1839 marked the beginning of over a decade of war, which was to extend the boundaries of British dominion to include Sind, the Punjab and large segments of Burma. But for the time being India was at peace. The anarchy of the eighteenth century was over; the issue of the struggle for

12

supremacy had been decided; and British hegemony was a *fait accompli*. It was widely believed that Indian wars were now a thing of the past; the stuff of history books and old soldiers' tales. 'The struggle which had thus ended in the universal establishment of British influence', wrote the historian Henry Prinsep after the third Anglo-Mahratta war of 1817, 'is particularly important and worthy of attention, as it promises to be the last we shall ever have to maintain with the native powers of India.'[3]

This notion had important social consequences, because it created a political climate in which the civil servant flourished and the military officer languished. Now that the process of acquiring an empire was thought to be over the prevailing concern was to vindicate its retention. The notion that India was the field of a moral mission — so eloquently expressed by Edmund Burke — became a powerful influence, and changed the object of British policy from the acquisition of tribute to the promotion of the happiness and prosperity of the Indian people. Evangelicalism and liberalism combined to ensure that Westernisation was the means adopted to this end, since the one engendered contempt for the customs and institutions of India while the other encouraged confidence and pride in those of Britain. The prevailing concern was to regenerate India through the introduction of Western technology and Western values, and so during the 1820s and '30s the British Indian government sponsored important developments in public works, English education and social reform. British civil servants found themselves encumbered with new demanding responsibilities and standards of competence and respectability. The 'District Officer', the characteristic agent of British administration, had, after much trial and experiment, finally emerged in all parts of British India save lower Bengal. Officially known as Magistrate and Collector,

13

he was the satrap of a domain that could be as much as 3,000 square miles in area with a population of up to a million people. He was not like the merchant adventurer of the old days, living in oriental luxury with Indian wife and olive-coloured children and amassing a fortune by private trading and venal abuses; but rather a clean-handed, sun-dried bureaucrat of the type portrayed by Kipling, labouring under a mountain of paper work, drawing a regular salary and striving to preserve Victorian social proprieties. Among these a white wife was the most essential, and to supply the need a marriage market had sprung up in Calcutta, which was regularly replenished with hopeful single females.

As the civilian administrator had come to the front of the stage, so the soldier had gone to the rear. With the advent of prolonged peace, military establishments had been reduced and regimental life had reverted to a humdrum routine of drill, changing stations and escorting treasure or convict working parties, enlivened by nothing more than the occasional big-game hunt, duck shoot or race meeting. It was a life from which every ambitious officer aspired to escape, by securing a political post or joining the General Staff. The old soldier of fortune, who knew his men, spoke their language, smoked his hookah and was kept on his toes by active service, had been replaced by a cigar-chewing, disgruntled professional – demoralized by idleness, seniority promotion and pay reductions, and venting his frustration by drinking, quarrelling and affecting to despise all things Indian. There was no room for the pious and high-minded in the Indian army of those days, as William Arnold (brother of Matthew) discovered with some pain. His experiences of army life inspired him to write *Oakfield*, a novel whose pessimistic message was that the British could not hope to civilize India until they had civilized themselves. The low moral tone and querulous discontent of the officer corps inevitably impaired the discipline and efficiency of the native ranks, and it is not surprising that it was the military part of the British system that finally collapsed in 1857.

Because of the haphazard and accidental nature of its growth, the British Raj was full of contradictions and strange anomalies. It was a marvel, really, that it existed at all. There was something freakish about it; something that defied probability and contingency. The British ruled directly a population of some ninety millions and protected an area of one and a quarter million square miles whose total population was probably in the region of 140 or 150 millions; yet in 1835 there were no more than 24,000 British civil servants, military officers and soldiers serving in India. The secret of their success lay in the loyalty of their native armies, of which there was one at each of the three Presidencies – making a total of 124,000 men – and in the lack of any sense of national identity amongst the linguistically distinct and politically divided Indian peoples, who did not know 'India' even as a word until they learnt it from the Europeans.

It was arguable that legally the British were not sovereign in the territories they ruled, since there was in Delhi, the old Imperial capital, a member of the Mughal dynasty who had never relinquished his claim to be Emperor. In theory, the native princes were his vassals and the British ruled the provinces of Bengal, Bihar and Orissa as his *diwan* or fiscal agent, by virtue of a grant bestowed on Robert Clive in 1765. In practice his power did not extend beyond the towering walls of the Red Fort, where he lived shut up with a host of indigent relatives, eking out a pension provided by the British and moving like a phantom amidst the ruins of former glory. To the British he was a tiresome anachronism, a symbol without meaning, and over the years they had gradually dropped the customary tokens of allegiance

15

and deference. They now recognised him only as King of Delhi and had replaced his image on their coins with that of their own monarch. In 1814 the British Governor-General, Lord Hastings, had refused to visit him because court etiquette demanded that he do so as an inferior; and in 1827 it had only been by promising that he would ask him to be seated that the King had persuaded Lord Amherst to pay a call. The dilapidated court of Delhi, with its tinsel favours and worthless trumpery, had become one of the sights of India, and no travel book was complete without an account of a visit to the 'Great Mogul' and some appropriate musing on the vicissitudes of fortune and the transience of wordly glory. There was little sympathy for the plight of the puppet king. The spirit of the age made people unresponsive to the pathos of fallen majesty and even subordinate officials had begun to resent having to show him any form of respect. Lieutenant Henry Edward Fane, Sir Henry's nephew and A.D.C., noted in his diary that he looked forward to his chief's visit to the King 'with disgust'. 'I did not like the General so lowering himself', he wrote, 'as to stand in the presence of a dirty, miserable old dog like this man, after having been seated in the durbar of Ranjit Singh.'[4]

There was further anomaly in the fact that the inhabitants of British India, although recognized in law as subjects of the British Crown, were in fact governed not by the Crown but by a chartered trading corporation, which held these territories in trust for it. This corporation was the East India Company, known to its Indian subjects as *jan kampani* ('the valiant Company') and thence by corruption as 'John Company' in popular English. The top officials in India, the Governor-General and Commander-in-Chief, were in effect (though not in theory) nominated by the British Government, and a government minister, the President of the Board of Control, had since 1784 managed the foreign and strategic policy of the Indian territories; but the headquarters of the Company, East India House in Leadenhall Street, were still the real nerve centre of the Indian empire, because this was where the purse strings were held and where most of the powers of appointment and dismissal resided. Here committees sat, debated, decided policy and drafted dispatches on matters relating to every aspect of the day-to-day administration of British India. Here thousands of documents arrived every year from the Indian presidencies, recounting the proceedings of the local governments in the minutest detail; and here, bound in wine-red leather volumes, they accumulated in one of the most remarkable and comprehensive archives in the world. Here, too, hundreds of hopeful young men, each duly nominated by a Company director and crammed by a specialist academy, presented themselves every year as candidates for civil and military employment in India.

The East India Company was organized like any other trading corporation. It had stockholders, dividends, directors and a chairman, and until 1842 its civilian employees were graded as Senior Merchants, Junior Merchants, Factors and Writers. It even retained a fleet of ships – the famous East Indiamen. But another chapter was added to the saga of paradox by the fact that it had completely abandoned trade. The Company had given up exporting to India after the withdrawal of its monopoly of the India trade in 1813 and had continued to import Indian silk, saltpetre and indigo, which were unprofitable, merely as a means of remittance. All the income from its Indian connections had since that date derived from land revenue, sales of opium (a government monopoly) and customs duties, and these failed to provide enough to cover the costs of administration and defence. For twenty years the Company had recouped some of its losses by trading with

China, selling Indian cotton goods at Canton and buying tea for sale at home. This had been an immensely profitable business; but in 1833 Parliament had required the Company to give up all its trading activities, and as a result of the winding-up of its China affairs its finances were in a parlous state. Throughout the 1830s it was having to make economies and retrenchments in every direction.

It was the Indian Mutiny of 1857–58 that finally knocked away the last props of public confidence in the East India Company and ensured the transfer of the government of British India to the Crown. But the Mutiny was the occasion, rather than the cause, of this devolution. Looking back, it seems clear that the Company's days were numbered in any case. Throughout the last half-century of its existence it had to battle against increasingly strong currents of opinion. Political economists denounced it as an affront to the doctrines of free trade and *laissez-faire.* Merchants and industrialists complained that its revenue policies were ruining the purchasing power of the Indian population. Reformers condemned it as an enclave of privilege and nepotism. Evangelicals abhorred the secular tone of its administration and resented its refusal to sponsor missionaries. Philanthropists insisted that its limited resources and narrow, mercantile outlook made it unequal to the responsibility of promoting the welfare of a vast Asiatic empire. Its critics judged it a failure, in fact, because it had failed to make India prosperous, Christian and uncorrupt, and over the years they had exacted a steady surrender of its privileges by way of atonement. In 1813 its monopoly of the India trade had been taken away and in 1833 its trading charter abolished. In 1833 too it had lost the power to restrict European emigration to India; and in 1853 their civil patronage was to be taken from the directors and vested in the President of the Board of Control, for distribution to candidates selected by public examination.

4. *Up the Country*

The capital of British India was Calcutta, in the Bengal Presidency. In a hundred years it had grown from a humble emporium on the flats of the Ganges delta into a cosmopolitan 'City of Palaces' with a population of some 300,000 and an impressive skyline of towers, spires, domes, and masts of shipping. In the European suburb of Chowringhee there were paved streets and handsome squares of town houses in the neo-classical style, with white stucco colonnades and green Venetian blinds; and on the Strand, every evening in the cold weather, the wealthy inhabitants paraded in britzkas, landaulettes, buggies, chariots and broughams, copied by local coachmakers from the latest models of Long Acre. Apart from one or two concessions to Indian convention – such as rising early to escape the heat and employing the huge number of servants prescribed by the functional caste system – there was little to distinguish the social life of the European governing and trading classes from that of their contemporaries in London or Cheltenham. The civilian and military communities involved themselves in a non-stop round of dinner parties, theatre and opera, balls, race meetings, charity sales and official functions; and the life of ladies was governed by the rituals of the morning call and evening reception. The gargantuan meals with which the British habitually gorged themselves acknowledged only a trifling debt to Indian cuisine. Curries and pilaus were perennially popular and mangoes were consumed greedily in season; but the staple menu was not much different from that of a well set-up table at home. Beef, mutton and veal were always available in the Calcutta bazaars and familiar vegetables

19

adapted happily to the local soil and climate. Delicacies not obtainable locally were imported by private traders, who had made it their special object, since the opening of the India trade in 1813, to supply the needs of the European community. The 'Europe shops' of Calcutta contained, according to one writer, 'all the stock to be found at Fortnum and Mason's'[5], including 'York and Westphalia hams, reindeer tongues, cheeses of all kinds, hermetically sealed vegetables and fish, anchovies and sardines, potted meats, German sausages, pickles, preserved fruits.' Familiar wines, especially madeira, champagne and claret, were in plentiful supply and English beer had made its appearance under the famous brand names of Hodgson, Bass, Allsop and Guinness. At about 1s 3d a bottle it was cheaper than at home and could now be drunk chilled, thanks to the new scheme of importing American ice. The social life of Calcutta could not satisfy those who, like Miss Roberts and Miss Fane, were fresh from the assembly rooms and theatres of fashionable London; they tended to find it philistine and drab – in a word, 'colonial'; but there was no denying that the city was the showpiece of British India, and many natives found there much to admire and imitate. The Nepalese general who features in the early pages of Isabella's letters is a case in point.

Calcutta was the seat of the Government of India, comprising the Governor-General (not called Viceroy until after the Mutiny) and his Council. It was to remain so until 1911, when the British began to transfer their central government to Delhi; but even as early as the 1830s the opinion was being voiced that the city was not suitable as an imperial capital. Its ethos was too mercantile and its position too peripheral. The northwestern frontier of the British territory had moved farther and farther away, until it was now a thousand miles from Calcutta and a delay of something like two months intervened before the government could get replies from the remoter stations. It was no longer possible to exercise close control over even the affairs of the Bengal Presidency from the capital, and the tour of inspection had consequently become an established part of governmental routine. As the distances were so large and the methods of transport so slow, these tours entailed long absences, and the splendid state apartments in Government House would often remain shuttered and dust-sheeted for years on end. The first of these extended viceregal tours had begun in June 1814, when Lord Hastings and his suite left Calcutta for the upper provinces with an army of clerks, secretaries and servants, and it had not ended until October the following year.

But the inconveniences of Calcutta were not only geographical. Its climate too was a lot less than ideal, and since it had become possible for the Governor-General to spend the summer somewhere cooler there had been an extra inducement to spin out absence from the capital. The cool retreat in question was Simla, 7,000 feet above the sea in the Himalayan foothills, in territory conquered from Nepal in 1815. By the 1830s it was already a thriving sanatorium and summer resort, with a bazaar, theatre, assembly rooms, metalled road, bridge, and numerous houses 'neatly and scientifically built of unmortared stone, intersected horizontally, at intervals of two feet, by pine beams dovetailed at the angles.'⁶ With its mountain breezes, rhododendron groves, deodar glades, alpine vistas and frosty nights, it was a blissful refuge from the torrid summers of the plains, and tours of inspection were timed so that the official party spent the cold weather travelling and visiting the lowland stations and arrived in Simla at the onset of the hot season in April. The first Governor-General to visit Simla was Lord Amherst, who by spending the summer of 1827 there had prolonged his absence from Calcutta to twelve months. Lord William

Bentinck, his successor, had made it a habit to spend about half the year on tour, passing the hot months either at Simla, where he had a special residence built, or at Utakanand in the Nilgiri hills, near the southern tip of the peninsula. Lord Auckland, who became Governor-General while the Fanes were in India, spent over two years away from Calcutta, from October 1837 until January 1840, and for five months of that period, during the summer and autumn of 1838, he was at Simla. Thereafter the absences of the Governors-General were to be even more prolonged. Writing in 1852, Sir George Campbell reckoned that holders of the office had spent only three out of the previous ten years in Calcutta.[7]

The Commander-in-Chief spent even less time in the capital. In fact he was hardly ever there, and his place on the Council was generally filled by a deputy. His absence, like the Governor-General's, was partly in the nature of his job. He had overall responsibility for the three native armies belonging to the Company, as well as for the forces of the Crown serving in India; but because it was the largest and strategically most important force, it was the Bengal Army that engaged his closest attention. This was scattered in detachments throughout the length and breadth of the Bengal Presidency, so extended tours were essential if adequate supervision was to be maintained. The military chiefs liked especially to keep an eye on the three divisions which garrisoned the 'upper provinces' beyond Benares (called the North-Western Provinces after 1834), with headquarters at Kanpur ('Cawnpore'), Meerut and Karnal, since these constituted a 'field army' and were supposed to be in a state of constant readiness for service. Sir George Nugent had made a prolonged tour in the cold weather of 1812–13 and his example had been followed by each of his successors. Again, the discovery of Simla had increased reluctance to return to Calcutta and Commanders-in-Chief patronized the hill station

22

even more than Governors-General did. Its attractions were doubly strong to them since they were, like Isabella's father, generally elderly and infirm generals, unaccustomed to the Indian climate and liable to wilt and sicken in the sticky heat of lower Bengal. Lord Combermere had set the precedent with a long visit to Simla, lasting from April till October, in 1828; and most of his successors had made it a habit to hurry away to the hills, *via* the up-country stations, almost as soon as they had arrived, taking with them all their aides, staff and office paraphernalia. Sir Henry Fane left Calcutta in September 1836, a year after his arrival, and never returned. The hot weather of 1837 and almost the whole of 1838 were spent at Simla, and during the remaining eighteen months of his period in India he was either on tours of inspection or at Bombay awaiting his passage home.

These top-brass visitations set a fashion, and by the mid-1830s that characteristic feature of British social life in India, the summer migration to the hills, had already become established. Henry Edward Fane wrote in his journal of a Simla 'season' lasting from May till October and attracting a temporary population of some 5,000 people.[8] It seems, too, that early Victorian Simla was as notorious for its scandal as was that of Kipling's day. That lady contributor to the *Calcutta Review* of 1845 wrote with prim disapproval of its effect on female morals:

> Society at our hill station partakes a good deal of the characteristics of a watering place or a garrison town in England; it consists for the most part of people who studiously leave behind them their habitual cares and employments, or of those who say they have nothing to do. Like causes produce similar results in all latitudes. Men who have several hours each day to get rid of naturally seek the society of any tolerably pretty and pleasant young woman, especially if her attractions are backed up by a good tiffin at two o'clock. Their attentions are agreeable

and gradually create a craving for this kind of stimulus; love of admiration involves petty jealousies, extravagant dress, paltry shifts and a thousand other evils, equally deteriorating to a woman's domestic character.[9]

Until the introduction of railways, in the 1860s, these official peregrinations followed the same stately routine. They necessitated living partly on board ship and partly under canvas. The first stages were by river transport up the Ganges, the main artery of communication in lower Bengal. In June 1814 Lord Hastings and his suite had embarked on 400 sailing barges, which took four months to travel the 900 miles to Kanpur. Frequent disembarkation for visits of inspection had held up progress on this occasion; but even at top speed this type of voyage used to take about three months. The vessel most frequently used was the 'budgerow' (from the Hindi *bajra*). This was a round-bottomed craft with a high poop, which, as it could only sail before the wind, often had to be tracked by the crew. Since then things had got quicker and less ostentatious. In October 1828, watched by crowds of curious and excited natives, the first steamboat to be seen at Allahabad had arrived from Calcutta, having covered the 800-mile distance in only twenty-six days. By the 1830s the government had brought a regular steam passenger service into operation, which cut the journey time to Allahabad to a month or even less. Mrs Fanny Parks appreciated the convenience, but regretted the loss of the old 'country' vessels on aesthetic grounds. 'The steamers answer well', she wrote; 'but what ugly-looking mercantile things they are!' The steamers were in fact tugs. The passengers travelled on towed 'flats' specially built for the service by Maudslay, Feild and Son, the London engineers. They were flat-bottomed, iron-plate shells, about 120 feet long and fifteen wide, surmounted by two decks. The living quarters were between decks, and the sides, instead of being flanked, were made of

Venetian blinds – one to each of about twenty cabins and two to the dining cabin, which stretched the full width of the vessel. Plate-glass windows were provided for use in the cold weather. Passengers could take the air on the upper deck, which was covered by canvas awning. Here too was the galley, with a cowhouse and hencoop to ensure fresh provisions during the voyage.[10] Isabella Fane's account of her river voyage in 1836 makes it clear that all was not plain sailing for these early steam vessels. Inexpert navigation led to groundings on mudbanks and collisions with native craft, and there were delays as the primitive engines battled in vain against strong contrary currents. The average speed on the upstream journey was only three and a half miles an hour.[11]

This mode of transport ruled out the long river retinues of Lord Hastings's day, since even as late as the early '50s there were only twelve government steamers in service. The procedure now was for the Governor-General or Commander-in-Chief to send on most of his baggage by 'country' vessels and the main part of his suite by road to a rendezvous at Allahabad or Kanpur, while he followed by river steamer with his family and personal staff. Sir Henry Fane had to make do with one tug and flat in 1836, and Lord Auckland with two the following year. Even Lord Dalhousie, never concerned to keep a low profile as Governor-General, was to use no more than three for his tour of 1849.

Members of the party who went overland travelled by 'dawk' (*dak*) or post carrier. There were no mail coaches until the 1840s, when the road from Calcutta to Kanpur was metalled. Conveyance was by means of a palanquin, a long box-like receptacle for one person, generally likened to a coffin on poles, which relays of coolies carried on their shoulders. Here is one traveller's description of this type of voyage:

You generally commence a dawk trip after dark and, habited in loose drawers and a dressing gown, recline at full length and slumber away the night. If you are wakeful, you may draw back the sliding panel of a lamp fixed behind, and read. Your clothes are packed in large neat baskets, covered with green oilcloth and carried.by palanquin boys. Two pairs will contain two dozen complete changes. Your palanquin is fitted up with pockets and drawers. You can carry in it, without trouble, a writing desk and two or three books and a few canteen conveniences for your meals; and thus you may be comfortably provided for many hundred miles' travelling. . . . The relays of bearers lie ready every ten or twelve miles; and the average of your run is about four miles an hour.[12]

Less comfortable, certainly, than gliding up the Ganges in a spacious Maudslay flat; but not, necessarily, any slower, since the meanderings of the river made the water route much longer. In 1827 Captain Mundy, a member of Lord Combermere's suite, had reached Kanpur from Calcutta in a month by travelling day and night, with only brief rests for meals and baths at the government 'dawk bungalows' along the route.[13]

Once the whole party had assembled and begun its camp life the years rolled back and progress continued with a mixture of oriental magnificence and oriental confusion, as Isabella's accounts vividly testify. Each member of the official party was assigned a lavish establishment of personal servants and animals. In 1827 Captain Mundy had had three tents, two elephants, six camels, four horses, a pony, a buggy and twenty-four servants, besides mahouts, camel drivers and tent pitchers. Lieutenant Henry Edward Fane tells us that during Sir Henry's tour his own establishment consisted of 'an elephant, four horses, eight camels and twenty domestics – a pretty handsome quantity for one individual'.[14] He estimated that the whole gathering, including escort and camp followers, amounted to 5,000 people, with four or five hundred camels and seventy or

26

eighty elephants. When the tents were pitched the camp was like a small town:

All the principal tents, that is those of the Commander-in-Chief, his personal and general staff, form a long street about fifty feet wide, the General's being always in the centre, the great durbar or dining tents on one side and the sleeping tents on the opposite. . . . Behind the lines of great tents are the 'routies' (a smaller kind of second tent for breakfast) and servants' tents; beyond which one's saddle horses and cattle stand picqueted. . . . At some little distance in rear of the main camp is that of the bazaar. Quite on the outskirts of all are picqueted the elephants and camels . . . and near them the long drilled lines of picqueted dragoon horses of the escort, with their officers' and masters' tents.[15]

5. *India and the Fane Family*

Like most prominent landowning families in the nineteenth century, the Fanes had numerous contacts with India – though they were not in any sense 'nabobs' (*nouveaux riches* who had made their money there). The first member of the family on record as having entered the service of the East India Company is Sir Henry's brother, William Fane, who was appointed Writer in 1805. By the time his brother and niece arrived in India he had risen to the rank of Senior Merchant and was serving on the Board of Revenue at Allahabad. Isabella and her father visited him during their stay at Allahabad in October 1836 and his daughter Caroline accompanied them to Kanpur. A distant kinsman of Isabella, William John Jarvis Fane, of the Fane family of Wormsley in Oxfordshire, had a tragically brief career in the military service of the Company. Shortly after being commissioned cornet in the Bengal Cavalry in 1826 he was invalided home and died at sea in July 1830. He was the first of three members of the family to die in this way. Both Isabella's uncle William and her father died

27

at sea during the return voyage from the East; the first in 1839 and the second a year later. Isabella's cousin, Henry Prinsep Fane, was appointed Writer in the Company's service in 1842 and remained in India throughout the Mutiny, when, as Magistrate of Jaunpur District, he made a daring escape from the rebels.

Several members of the family served in India as officers in the royal army. Most prominent among them was of course Sir Henry himself. Grandson of the eighth and nephew of the tenth Earl of Westmorland, he was a Peninsular War veteran and close friend of the Duke of Wellington. It was at the suggestion of the Duke, serving as Foreign Secretary in Sir Robert Peel's short ministry of 1834–5, that he was appointed Commander-in-Chief in India. In his younger days Sir Henry had been known as 'the handsome A.D.C.', and at sixty he still cut a dashing figure. 'He is a magnificent looking man', wrote Mrs Parks, 'with a good soldier-like bearing; one of imposing presence, a most superb bow and graceful speaking.' But he was not robust, and his poor health was a constant source of concern to his devoted daughter. The two Henrys of Isabella's letters, one Sir Henry's son and the other (Henry Edward) his nephew, were both King's (later Queen's) officers serving as A.D.C.s to the Commander-in-Chief. Their kinsman, Frank Fane, was serving Governor-General Lord Dalhousie in the same capacity in 1851, when he succeeded to the title of Earl of Westmorland. Mildmay Fane, another of Isabella's uncles, served briefly in India as a major-general in 1854; and her cousin, Francis Augustus Fane, did two spells of duty there: first as General Mildmay Fane's A.D.C., and then during the Mutiny as the raiser and commander of a regiment of irregular horse.

Most of these men, and many of their wives and womenfolk, were prolific diarists and correspondents. The selection that follows is only a sample from a legacy

28

of documentary material that richly illustrates what is still one of the least known aspects of the British historical experience.

Notes

1 Emma Roberts, *Scenes and Characteristics of Hindustan*: London, 1837, i, pp.56–7; ii, p.26.
2 Emily Eden, *Letters from India*: London, 1872, i, p.128.
3 Henry T. Prinsep, *History of the Political and Military Transactions in India during the Administration of the Marquis of Hastings:* London, 1825, ii, p.418.
4 H.E. Fane, *Five Years in India*: London, 1842, i, p.262.
5 J.H. Stocqueler, *India: Its History, Climate, Productions:* London, 1857, pp.64–5.
6 George Mundy, *Pen and Pencil Sketches*: London, 1832, i, p.227. See also George Francis White, *Views in India*: London, 1838, pp.72–5.
7 George Campbell, *Modern India*: London, 1852, p.218.
8 Fane, op.cit., i, pp.215–6.
9 *Calcutta Review*, vol. 4, p.114.
10 *Household Words,* April 26th, 1853.
11 H. Bernstein, *Steamboats on the Ganges*: Bombay, 1960, p.85.
12 Anon., *Sketches of India Written by an Officer for Fireside Travellers at Home*: London, 1824, pp.218–9.
13 Mundy, op. cit.
14 Fane, op. cit., i, p.54.
15 Ibid., i, pp.58–60.

Biographical Notes

AUCKLAND, Lord George Eden, Earl of Auckland, 1784–1849. Served as President of the Board of Trade and Master of the Mint in the 'Reform' Whig ministry of 1830–34. Governor-General of India 1836–42. Associated most especially with the disastrous first Afghan War, Auckland has always been regarded as one of the least distinguished viceroys. His reputation never recovered from the indictment in Sir John Kaye's *History of the War in Afghanistan* (1851). Kaye depicted him as a weak, irresolute character acting at the behest of strong-headed and misguided subordinates – especially the three secretaries who accompanied him on his upcountry tour (Henry Torrens, John Colvin and William Macnaghten). Sir Auckland Colvin, in his biography of his father (*John Russell Colvin*, Oxford 1895) revealed that Kaye had over-emphasized the role of the secretaries and that the Afghan policy was in fact dictated by the ministry in London; but his evidence did nothing to modify Kaye's assessment of Auckland's personality. All contemporary informants (including Isabella Fane) agree that Auckland seemed pathologically shy and unnerved by the responsibilities of his office, and his despatches suggest a muddled and even inarticulate man. It is hardly open to doubt that such a person would have been very much under the influence of a dominant character like John Colvin, whose imperious manner earned him the nickname 'King John'.

BERESFORD, Marc Colonel, later General, Marcus Beresford, 1800–1876. Nephew of the second Baron Decies. Served as Military Secretary to Sir Henry Fane. His first wife, Isabella (née Sewell) died in 1836. He

30

married his second wife, Caroline Fane (q.v.), in 1838. Like Isabella and H.E. Fane he kept a journal while in India, and this is now in the India Office Records.

CAROLINE ('CARRY')   See under FANE

CHRISTINE   Isabella's sister-in-law. Wife of her brother, Major Henry Fane.

EDEN, *the Misses* Emily and Frances (Fanny), younger sisters of Lord Auckland. Emily (1797–1869) was a prominent figure in Whig society and had reputedly once been wooed by Lord Melbourne, the Whig Prime Minister. Later she achieved some fame as an authoress. An anthology of her letters from India was published in 1866 under the title *Up The Country*, and further selections were printed after her death (*Letters from India*, 1872; *Miss Eden's Letters*, 1919). She also wrote two novels (*The Semi-detached House,* 1859, and *The Semi-attached Couple,* 1860), which enjoyed considerable popular success. She was an accomplished artist, and prepared a portrait of Queen Victoria for official presentation to Ranjit Singh in 1838. A selection of engravings from her sketches appeared in 1844 under the title *Portraits of the People and Princes of India.*

FANE, *Caroline* Isabella's cousin. Second daughter of William Fane (see Introduction, Section 5). She became the second wife of Marc Beresford (q.v.) in 1838.

——, *Henry* (i) Major, later Colonel, Henry Fane (1802–1885). Eldest son of Sir Henry Fane. Acted as A.D.C. to his father in India, and inherited the family estate at Fulbeck after his death. Like all Sir Henry's children, he was illegitimate, and does not therefore figure in Burke's *Landed Gentry*.

——, *Henry* (ii) Lieutenant Henry Edward Fane. Isabella's cousin. Nephew and A.D.C. to Sir Henry Fane. In 1842 he published an account of his experiences in the East under the title *Five Years in India*.

——, *Sir Henry* See Introduction, *passim*

——, *William* See Introduction, Section 5

HENRY See under FANE

JOHN See under MICHEL

MARC See under BERESFORD

METCALFE, *Sir Charles* Charles Theophilus, Baron Metcalfe, 1785–1846. One of the most distinguished and talented members of the East India Company's civil service. He acted as provisional Governor-General after the departure of Lord William Bentinck in 1835. His appointment to the permanent Governor-Generalship was vetoed by the Whig cabinet in London, ostensibly because it was not the tradition to appoint Company employees to this high office, but in reality probably because Metcalfe was opposed to the 'forward' policy in central Asia favoured by the government. He was appointed to the newly created Lieutenant-Governorship of the North-Western Provinces in 1836 and resigned the Company's service in 1838, after being passed over for the vacant Governorship of Madras. In the last years of his life he was consecutively Governor of Jamaica and Governor-General of Canada. Metcalfe was never married in the British legal sense, but he lived for many years with an Indian consort, by whom he had three sons. Evidence suggests that she was a Sikh lady met during a diplomatic mission to Ranjit Singh's court in

1809; but nothing certain is known of her, since all documents relating to this aspect of Metcalfe's life were destroyed after his death by a morbidly sensitive sister. The racial discrimination of British Indian society prevented her (if still alive) from assuming her rightful role as Metcalfe's hostess. She consequently makes no appearance in contemporary journals and letters and Lady Ryan, wife of the Chief Justice of Bengal, was acknowledged as the head of Calcutta society. But her existence was apparently known. Metcalfe himself made no secret of his sons and it seems obvious from one of Isabella's remarks that his romantic and unorthodox liaison was a common topic of gossip. 'Sir C.', she tells her aunt, 'has the reputation of not caring for [i.e. caring about] colour in his little amours'.

MICHEL, *John* Captain, later Field-Marshal Sir John Michel, 1804–1886. Nephew of Sir Henry Fane, being the son of his sister Anne. Acted as Sir Henry's A.D.C. and subsequently served with distinction in the Kaffir wars, in India, in the Crimea and in China. Knighted in 1858 for his part in the supression of the Mutiny in central India. Married Louisa Churchill in May 1838.

PRINSEP, *Thoby and Mrs* Henry Thoby Prinsep, 1792–1878. East India Company civil servant and accomplished oriental scholar. Appointed Persian Secretary to the Indian government in 1820, and member of the Supreme Council in 1835. Became a director of the Company after his retirement in 1848. In the education debate of the 1830s he opposed those (led by Macaulay) who advocated government sponsorship of English education to the exclusion of traditional learning. He disapproved of the official Afghan policy and formed a low estimate of Auckland's professional capabilities.

His wife, Sarah (1816–87), whom he married in 1835, was one of the celebrated Pattle sisters, a bevy of seven daughters including Lady Somers, Lady Dalrymple and Julia Margaret Cameron, the famous photographer (who makes two appearances in the letters). Their father was

James Pattle, a rich and notorious Indian adventurer nicknamed Jemmy Blaze, who died in Calcutta in 1845. After their return from India the Prinseps took the lease of Little Holland House, and for twenty-five years presided there over one of London's best known *salons*. The aspiring and the distinguished from all walks of life used to gather at Mrs Prinsep's on Sunday afternoons from 1850 until 1875.

RUNJEET Maharaja Ranjit Singh. See Introduction, Section 2

THE LETTERS OF ISABELLA FANE

PART ONE: CALCUTTA

I

Saturday January 2nd, 1836   I sincerely trust, my dear
Mrs Chaplin, when this reaches you it will have found
you in the enjoyment of all the happiness I should have
wished you had you been near me at this time.

Mrs Beresford and I, John, and Henry and Captain
Campbell all went to the Italian opera. I had made a
vow I never would go again, it was so bad and I was so
bored the first time I went; but there was an amateur
performer whose musical talents were said to be very
great, and my curiosity was excited in consequence.
The opera was the *Barbiere* [either Rossini's or
Paesiello's *Il Barbiere di Siviglia*]. Fortunately, I have not
been in the way of many operas in England, therefore I
could not draw comparisons between a Pasta, a Sontag,
etc., etc., and our frightful squeakers. Had it not been
for Mr Torrens,★ the amateur, it would have been as
intolerable as the former occasion, and although I was
amazingly disappointed in him, as far as his singing
went, his acting was beautiful and the failure in the
former respect proceeded from his voice not being
sufficiently powerful to fill the house. In a room, no
doubt, it would be very different. If you could but have
seen the Rosina he had to make love to! In point of size

★ Henry Whitelocke Torrens, East India Company's civil service. At
this time Officiating Secretary to Government in the General and
Financial Departments. Later one of the notorious secretaries who
accompanied Auckland on his up-country tour.

she is exactly poor darling Mrs Fane of Wimpole Street, without any of her good points, for she is the same huge size all the way down and her legs and feet are never to be forgotten.★ The masts of a man of war are a joke to the former and the latter are more like an elephant's squeezed into shoes than anything else, and this was Rosina! The house was very full, and it was not at all hot. There was a figure in the pit which afforded us much amusement. It was a character known here by the appellative of bearer. These creatures make the beds, dust the rooms and perform all such offices. These beauties wear nothing in the shape of clothes but a dirty piece of coarse (intended to be white) cloth, in which they envelope the whole of their person (even their head in this inclement weather), leaving nothing out but their eyes. A figure of this sort, I suppose he must have had a musical turn, came into the pit actually holding on by the skirts of a half-caste's coat. Down he squatted himself on one bench, with his chin resting upon another, and during the whole of the performance he never stirred, but appeared lost in amaze or pleasure or some undefinable feeling.

Monday 4th   This morning I went to pay a visit or two with Mrs Beresford, to two ladies who sail tomorrow for England, one for her health; and we flattered ourselves with the hope that there would be an end of her, for her husband is one of those who hold such a situation that when we move up the country, so will he, bag and baggage, and we thought what a blessed thing that by her departure we should be spared so much; but yesterday, to my horror and amaze, I found she intended to return by the ship in which she goes, ready

★ This was probably Mme St. Nesoni. See Emily Eden's *Letters*, i, p. 107.

to go up to the hills with us when we start. However, she will have deposited all her bairns, which will be a good portion of rubbish out of the way. Mrs Elliott we also went to bid adieu to, but the gates were shut, which means not at home here, so I did my duty at small cost. I also went to try and see and laugh at Mrs Thobias *fool* Prinsep. She is decidedly in that way in which ladies 'like to be who love their Thobys' and the fuss they both make about it is truly droll and nasty. *He tells* young and old. Upon my honour, he with his very own lips and in plain English has told both me and John of her *situation*, and she by her nonsensical airs and graces takes care all the world should know her share in the business.

Wednesday 6th Two morning visitors in the shape of two of the A.D.C.s from Government House. Poor creatures, their reign is nearly at an end, and very much they will feel the change of things here. Sir C. Metcalfe is a most amiable, kind-hearted man; much given to favouritism, and upon all the men upon his staff he *heaps* favours, so that when Lord Auckland comes, if he does, they will all go to the right about. My father is so much better that we had in addition to our own party four old military fograms to dinner and we went, all of us excepting him, to a big ball at Government House. Conceive what a set of A.D.C.s ours are. Henry is the one who sends out the invitations. On this occasion he invites the Beresfords and leaves out her brother, who is staying with her! Secondly, it is the duty of the acting A.D.C. for the week to see that the carriage is ready whenever wanted, and to order it at the proper hour. Last night John (being the one on duty) never thought about it until about half an hour before it was time to start for the ball. In this country none of the servants is either victualled or slept. Our coachman's house was a great way off, and he could not be got at in time. The close carriage was also not to be got at, so in consequence of all this idleness Christine and I were obliged, at one o'clock in the morning, to come home from the ball in the open carriage, in a heavy and unwholesome fog, with one of those idle fellows to drive us.

Thursday 7th   We had a long visit in the morning from Mr Saunders, a very old friend of the W. Fanes. He is going to England at the end of this month after a residence here of 25 years without setting his foot on the shores of England once during that time. He is a very good specimen, proving that India may agree, for he is fat, jolly and good-humoured, and says during all these number of years he has had no illness worth mentioning. They say there is a young widow trying hard to detain him, or at least that he shall not go home a widower, which at present he is, with three bairns at home. She must make haste for he sails on the 28th.

Friday 8th   I had to entertain all by myself our morning visitors, a General and Mrs Watson: the former a nice old man, but his wife a dreadful stick; but, poor thing, she had just lost a married daughter when we arrived, after an illness of a few hours, and yesterday was of course in deep mourning, and appeared very depressed in spirits. It was a delicious cold day, and my feet throughout the whole of it as cold as stones, the same exactly as they used to be in England. I do not like them to be so, for fear of the pain in my heart, which has been so well ever since I have been in India, excepting during my confinement from the musquito wounds.

Saturday 9th   We have all put into the lottery,* and amongst us have purchased three tickets. We are all building our hopes on fortune, but in a day or two you will hear the result.

Sunday 10th   John and I only went to church. I daily expect to hear that the Calcutta folks have changed their minds, and that they will say John is to be my husband, and not Sir C. Metcalfe! We had a new and such a preacher. Not a syllable he said could one hear, he preached in so shrill a tone of voice, and exactly as if he were crying all the time. We dined at home, the Beresfords only in addition to our own party, and went to bed very early, *viz* half-past nine, because on Monday 11th we had to get up so early to attend the Calcutta races, and the first race began at seven o'clock. It would be impossible to make you believe, I am sure, the wonderful coldness of the morning. Although I had on warm things I was so cold in the stand that Mrs Beresford and I determined to go outside, to be in the sun. I need not enumerate all the things people wear in winter in England, for all these I had, but in addition a lined satin pelisse; under that one of those double knitted lambswool tippets; a large shawl; a boa; and a pair of trowsers extra – and yet I was perished! Could

---

* Victor Jacquemont wrote about this lottery in the early 1830s: 'I may say that there is a lottery at Calcutta every six months, with 6,000 tickets costing 128 rupees each, so arrange that only a twelfth part of the sum subscribed for tickets remains in the bank. This sum serves to cover the expenses of various charitable institutions. But that is only a pretext to sanctify the gambling and enable the pious to take part in it, which they all do, and the impious as well. The number of civil and military officers in the whole of India amounts to about 6,000, the same as the tickets. There are few who do not voluntarily impose this tax of 128 rupees upon themselves from the day they arrive in India to the day they leave it.' (*Letters From India,* translated by C.A. Phillips: London, 1936, p.275).

you have believed this possible in India? From twelve to four it is hot; but at half past four when we go out for our drive it is again quite cold. We got home to breakfast by nine o'clock and we were altogether well amused. The racing, I believe, to those who understood anything about it, was not worth looking at; but I do not, so did very well, as we had little lotteries, and this created a small anxiety. I do not understand why the races here are not superior to all others. In England the *beau ideal* of a fine horse is an Arab, I fancied, and as every horse almost is an Arab, who should not the races be perfect? There was not nearly so large a concourse of spectators as at the review. I suppose Blackee is more military than sporting. I stood next in the stand to one of Tippoo's* sons, so I made a few observations to him. He speaks English very well and has very nice manners. He was dressed thus: a pair of Europe Wellington boots; a pair of dark blue cloth trowsers, just the same as our gentlemen wear; a beautiful tunic of kincob; and vest of another pattern kincob. His cap I could not describe, it is so peculiar and ugly, but all Tippoo's sons wear the same. I live on the hope that in consequence of this civility he may send me a present of a something. I mean *with this view* to speak to him upon every opportunity!

Tuesday 12th   In the evening we went to a musical entertainment at the house of Parker, Plowden & Co. One pays for going, although all the performers nearly are amateurs. The money goes to some charity, I forget what. I cannot say I was particularly amused, but I am not fond of Italian squalling even when well done, and when the performance is only middling it becomes a

---

* Tipu Sultan, ruler of Mysore. Defeated and killed by the British at Seringapatam in 1799. His family were made state pensioners.

greater bore still. I was therefore very glad at half-past eleven o'clock to get away. My father went to it, his first appearance in public since his illness. He has not yet left off his wraps, the swelling is not quite gone.

Friday 15th   A great event occurred on this day, *viz* the arrival of the Nepaul General* and an immense retinue. He is a man with a very enquiring mind and he has come to Calcutta to see the world, as well as to pay some compliment about unfurling a flag, the rights of which I don't quite understand. He was to land at half-past four in the afternoon, and we of course all resolved to see the fun.

Mrs Beresford and I sallied forth in the carriage in proper time to the landing place; but we found if we remained there and in the carriage we should see nothing, so we pushed through the crowd, little caring about the chances of knocking down Blackee like ninepins, until we arrived at the house of an acquaintance whose verandah we intended to invade, where we knew we should have a beautiful view; and so indeed we had. It was close to the backs of the river upon which part of the sight took place. The steamer took his boat in tow (which was a Government boat, for he and his troops marched the whole way from their territories), and his troops were in little boats around him. All the way down the river they kept up an incessant firing of musketry, which had an exceedingly

---

* Martabar Singh Thapa, sent on a complimentary visit by his uncle Bhim Sen Thapa, prime minister of Nepal. The Thapa family was prominent in Nepalese politics in the first decades of the nineteenth century, until the fall of Bhim Sen in 1839. After his return to Kathmandu in March 1836 Martabar Singh had a chequered career involving imprisonment, exile and finally (1843) a term of office as prime minister and commander-in-chief. He was assassinated in 1845.

pretty effect. He was taken in the steamer down to the fort, which fired a salute, and he then came back to the ghaut, or landing place. In the meantime we hurried down to our carriage, where we should have the best view of the rest of the exhibition. The troops then began to disembark, with their wild music playing, which was indescribable, and formed close to our carriage a long line two deep. An alley was left for the General to pass up, which he did in a carriage, accompanied by one of the A.D.C.s belonging to the Governor-General, his two little children, and someone else. His officers rode on beautifully caparisoned horses, so that we saw *them* to great advantage. The troops were a small race of men, but stout and sturdy looking, and are famous for their bravery and good discipline. They carried muskets with, instead of bayonets, a most formidable looking weapon shaped like a curved knife, and in their belts another fearful looking weapon. A house is taken for him about a mile from Calcutta, and his men are encamped round about him.

Well, we all went to the opera, and so did he, and sat in the next place to us. The opera boxes here are exactly upon the same construction as the dress circle in our theatres in London, so that he sat next to us with only a bar between. You never saw such a beautiful man, or anything so magnificent as his dress. He is tall and extremely well-made; not very dark, no beard, but a nice pair of long moustaches. If I could but describe his dress to you! I must try. I will begin with his head, on which he wore a framed turban, i.e., I mean one not twisted on. This was composed of gold-looking stuff, such as the material Mrs Fane sent home for turbans. This was done all over in patterns of beautiful pearls. He had in front an immense aigrette of diamonds, from the point of which dangled an immense emerald. He wore a rich purple velvet tunic-shaped coat, with a quantity of sable about it. The whole of the breast was a mass of

44

gold, which was again thickly covered with patterns in beautiful pearls, and in the centre of each pattern some precious stone. The sleeve of this vest ended at his elbow, and below came a shirt that was both curious and beautiful. It was composed of exceedingly fine muslin with a pink spot upon it, and would have made a lovely gown for any of us. A frill of the same peeped out of his frontispiece. His trowsers were of beautiful gold tissue, and his shoes magnificently embroidered. He wore a pair of European military epaulettes, but with this in addition, *viz* a long fringe of bullion which hung down below his elbow. His pocket handkerchief was of crimson gauze embroidered in gold. He has brought down his two sons with him, little boys, who were also very fine, but not to be compared to their father. One is very ugly, the other not at all so, and they both speak English a little. I was so astonished at his behaviour during the opera; if he had been brought up at the court of St. James's his manners could not have been better. He did not seem the least at a loss what to do, but sat on his chair like a gentleman and between the acts stood up and talked to those who could enter into conversation with him. Although he could not understand the least, of course, of what was going on, he did not appear the least bit sleepy, but said he was much amused at the novelty of the scene. I will not say more of him at present, for no doubt I shall have much more to tell you in the course of my journal. We were horridly bored at the opera. It was called *I Baccanali di Roma* [by Guiseppe Niccolini], and I believe no one ever heard of it before. The music would have been pretty if well sung, but our opera is beyond endurance.

Monday 18th   The morning so cold I shook so much that I could hardly eat my breakfast. At eleven o'clock I went with Mrs Beresford to pay some visits, amongst them to Mrs Holroyd, who has been very ill with a cold and small cholera. She is getting about but looked very much pulled down by it. She is such a very nice person. There was a large dinner at Government House, which was given to a bride. If you could but form a notion of the formality of one's entré. A huge room and a huge circle; Sir Charles Metcalfe stepping forward, giving you his fat arm and leading you to a seat; the women all in a circle and the men ditto. And so we had to sit until dinner was said to be ready. I got between two men who were talkative and agreeable, one a surgeon, a very gentlemanlike man - but is it not funny that the élite society of this place should be this sort? The other was Mr Torrens. I thought we never should have left the table. The lady who was to make the move was half asleep I believe, and sat and sat until we were worn to fiddlesticks mentally and bodily. We went for a few minutes to our Almack's.* The Nepaul General was there, much disgusted, I am told, with so much female exhibition. It was his own fault, he need not have gone. We were doing nothing contrary to our habits and if he could not reconcile his mind to it he had better have staid at home. He is said to have fixed his eyes most intently on Mrs Beresford – we have not yet ascertained whether in admiration or disgust. She has a beautiful bust which she generally displays more than she need, and on this occasion it was most conspicuous. So we think he might have been turning over in his mind that she would make him a capital nautch girl!

Tuesday 19th We had a large dinner party this evening, the Governor-General amongst the lot. I never was more bored than during the meal. It fell to my lot to be handed in by and to have to sit on one side of Sir Charles. I would not have felt in the least afraid of him if

* An exclusive London club, the hub of fashionable society, which met in Willis's Rooms, King Street, St. James's.

he had talked to me; but although he is good humour personified, and will bow and shake hands even *more* than he need, yet he is not a pleasant neighbour at a dinner, for he has no small talk. I have no doubt his mind is too great for *my* mind. I was so unfortunate as to be similarly situated on the other side, for *there* was perched Sir E. Ryan, the Supreme Judge, or something very learned; and although he has two detestable British daughters and a son enough to make ten dogs sick fron conceit, besides little children, yet he is either mighty wise or mighty postiche also. No doubt had you been me you would have found the neighbours pleasant, for *you could* have talked wisdom. I cannot.

Wednesday 20th   Sat at home as usual and worked all the morning. Rode out in the evening with my father, and ended the day with the play. We had first a droll thing called *One, Two, Three, Four,* in which a man took off Mathews and W. Farren [popular comic actors] very well. Afterwards we had *Pizarro* [Sheridan's adaptation of Kotzebue's *Der Spanier in Peru*], which was beyond their powers. The house was so full, and the Nepaul General was expected, but did not go. In spite of the concourse of people the house was not at all hot, but I am afraid we are coming to the end of our cool weather.

Thursday 21st   This morning the Nepaul General went in state to Government House and the Governor-General held what is called a durbar, that is, court. We ladies wanted very much to be hid away somewhere to see the show, but there was no place where we could hide, and as the sight of women is so contrary to their notions of propriety, Sir C. Metcalfe would not let us be admitted. The General presented his presents on the

47

occasion. I do not know what they all consisted of, but there were some for the King of England, and some for my father, alack, alas, which I hope we shall never even look upon; it will be so tantalizing to think that no one but Government will benefit by them.* Among the presents for the Governor-General there was a tiger which has been nursed and brought up by a woman. Woman and all is presented I believe. As Sir C. has the reputation of not caring for colour in his little amours she may prove an acceptable present. Our new A.D.C. is *hors-de-combat* with something wrong in his liver. We like him very much; he is gentlemanlike in his manners and unassuming, but has such a Scotch twang and puts one a little too much in mind of Sir M. Wallace.

Friday 22nd   I spent such an idle wandering life all on account of the Nepaul General, who was to come for a durbar here; but after it was so agreed there arose a difficulty because he would not take off his shoes at the door of my father, and unless he did he could not be received. The affair was arranged and at half-past three he came with a few of his Gourkas [Gurkhas] on horseback, himself in a carriage accompanied by his son and the Englishman who goes about with and takes care of him. He is a Dr Campbell, and is Surgeon of that Residency. He staid about 20 minutes, but what he said, or did, or wanted goodness knows, for I don't. He had attar poured over his handkerchief and paun [pan] (a thing they all eat here, which is betel nut and a leaf rolled up together and which makes the tongue and lips a deep scarlet) stuffed into his mouth – or rather presented to him to stuff in himself; and then he put his

---

* The acceptance of private gifts from natives by Company servants had been prohibited by the Regulating Act of 1773. Where etiquette demanded, gifts were still received, but they were treated as public property.

head on each side of my father's head and away he went. We all went out riding, and in the evening Henry and Christine and I and John went to Mrs Goodall Atkinson's concert of sacred music, which was too great a bore. She sang very well but the accompaniment spoilt all. The musquitoes were so numerous and wearing that even had the entertainment been better it would have been scarcely worth while to have endured their torture on any terms. The Nepaul General was there, and sat next to us.

Saturday 23rd   At half-past seven this morning there was a military spectacle for the Nepaul General. When we arrived at the ground there was such a dense fog we could not see a yard before us and it continued unfortunately long. I believe the manoeuvres were done to the great dissatisfaction of *our* General, and it is supposed the foreign one thought the men but slow coaches. He rode such a beautifully caparisoned horse. The saddle cloth was gold and looked studded with something like lapis lazuli. He looks remarkably well on horseback. We had his son in the carriage with us all the time, but he understands so very little English that beyond staring at him he afforded little amusement.

Monday 25th   A dreadful morning for me, for we have resolved to give a musical entertainment for the purpose of entertaining the Nepaul General, so I had to go and pay visits to make love to two amateur performers whose services I required. If I had had my choice, I would much rather have been hanged. Thank goodness, none were at home, so I wrote notes, which I did not mind half so much. There was a concert at Government House in the evening, which was honoured with our company for a very short time, for the public singers and the orchestras here are quite intolerable.

Tuesday 26th   There was an artillery review at a place about eight miles from Calcutta at four o'clock this afternoon, to which we also went. It was exceedingly worth seeing. The Nepaul General was there, and was very much delighted and astonished at all he saw. The manoeuvering of troops is not at all wonderful to him; his own can do the same; but anything to do with huge guns is quite out of his line. It was so droll to see the meeting and parting between him and my father. The proceeding is to put their cheeks together, first one then the other, not quite in close contact, but nearly. The crowds of spectators were inconceivable, chiefly natives, and the dust – you may suppose what it was when I tell you that the Epsom race dust was a joke to it. We went to a ball in the evening, one of the best we have been to in Calcutta. We staid but a short time, although for a wonder both Christine and I could willingly have remained longer, but my father wished to go and we did not like to keep him.

Wednesday 27th   Today the Nepaul General took his turn and gave us a military exhibition. It was a very pretty sight indeed, and all the military men said their manoeuvering was beautiful. Is it not singular that every word of command is given in English? At the end of the show the General made his troops form a square and in the midst he dismounted and saluted my father, which was a great compliment, and from one who hesitated about unshoeing himself, particularly flattering.

Thursday 28th   Today we all took our departure from Calcutta, to spend a couple of days at

50

Barrackpore.★ We embarked with the Governor-General, on board his boat, in tow of a steamer, at half-past one, and reached Barrackpore at about four. This is my first visit to it, as on a previous excursion my father made I was laid up with my musquito bites, and Christine also was in her bed, with her baby. Now we are both sound. It is a beautiful place; the park is so very pretty and looks so very English. A part is laid out in a very pretty flower garden. Another is appropriated to birds and beasts in dens; but at present the only inhabitants of these are a leopard and a tiger which the Nepaul General brought the other day, and two hippopotami – one brought by him also, the other has been here some time. Immediately upon our arrival the elephants were brought for us to ride upon if we liked, and although I had been longing for a ride upon one I must own the sight of them made me consider whether I would go or not. I am not naturally a coward, therefore I soon determined I would; so down knelt the elephant, up went the ladder, and then up mounted Christine and I in one, Mrs Beresford and child and an A.D.C. in another, and we set off to make the tour of the park. I was agreeably surprised in the motion of the huge brute. I was told the shaking was not to be described, but so far from finding it so I have *walked* on many a horse that has shaken me more; indeed, I am not sure that my darling Titus [a donkey] at Fulbeck was not quite as rough!

Friday 29th   This morning there was a review of upwards of 3,000 men, native regiments, and as we females always go wherever we can, we resolved not to be left behind. So we mounted our elephants, Mrs Beresford and I; Christine was on horseback. There was such a dreadful fog we could not see a yard before us –

★ The Governor-General's country residence.

which was particularly unlucky, for this was the largest body of men and best review we have yet been at out of the many we have already attended. But then we met with a frightful adventure which compensated for a great deal. Our elephant took fright at the firing, *whisked* round with us and then set off at a very quick shuffle and became unmanageable. Fortunately, as he got out of the alarming sound of the firing he attended to the violent poking the mirahoot [mahout] gave his unfortunate head with the weapon they carry to guide and manage them, and he then again became quite docile. But it was by no means a pleasant situation to be in. Mrs Beresford was horribly frightened and screamed aloud. I am not so easily alarmed, but still did not relish its conduct. The review was over by half-past nine and we actually saw nothing but the marching by, which was the finale. It is curious to see how little the horses in that neighbourhood cared for these moving mountains. For the marching past we on our great creature stood close behind the staff and none of their horses cared a pin about us.

The house at Barrackpore will only accommodate nine individuals, but there are several bungalows around the house – such nice little snug places, that look just like – ah! I know how to give you an idea of them; they are just like Mr King's cottage near you, but not so nice. They each contain a sitting room, two sleeping apartments and a little bath room. Christine and Henry and child had one; Mrs Beresford, husband and child another. My sleeping apartment was in the great house. Fancy what an odd country this is, and all the retinue each person is obliged to have about him. *I* could not go with less than two women and one man; Christine could not do with less than three women and three men; and as for my father, he had so many I could scarcely count them! Notwithstanding all this they give one no trouble about bed or board but sleep on the floor without bed or bedding, in the house or out of the house, as best may suit.

Saturday 30th   We left Barrackpore today at 12 o'clock in the same nice boat in tow of the steamer, only ourselves, and reached Calcutta about half-past three. I amused myself both going and coming by watching for pieces of dead bodies floating by us. I need not tell you, who read so much, of the sacred nature of the river and how throwing their dead into it is the native means of disposing of them, either burnt to ashes or whole and entire. My curiosity (laudable!!) was satisfied, for I saw many good specimens – particularly on our return, for one fine whole man floated past the window of the cabin at which I was standing, within half a yard. We regretted much our visit was so short, but we were obliged to return on this day as we had a large dinner – twenty-two we had, and it went off very well. We were very glad when they all said good-bye, notwithstanding its success.

Sunday 31st   Nothing but church. After that a visit to Thoby Prinsep. Poor old Thoby has been very ill for the last three weeks – but I told you so before. He has now been without fever for a week, and flatters himself he will be about again soon. He is ordered to the Sandheads★ for change of air and, I believe, means to go. We did not stay five minutes, thank goodness. Mrs Thoby I am sorry to say is out and about again. Her family way is going on all right, so now my peace and happiness are again destroyed as we shall have her in our train everywhere – the more so as she is not going with

---

★ A region in the Bay of Bengal, beyond the sandbanks at the mouth of the Hughli river.

her Thoby to the Sandheads for fear of accident in her interesting situation. I have called upon Mrs William Prinsep, who has recently arrived from England. She is a very pretty woman, but what very disagreeable manners she has! They tell me her husband makes more noise than all the Prinseps besides put together. God help us, if he beats James alone he is my horror. Think of there being five of the name now in Calcutta, three married and the wives running a race with each other who is to be confined first! Alas! our cold weather is gone. People are calling out about the heat. I do not feel it unpleasantly at all; the only way it affects me is by making my legs and feet swell.

Monday February 1st   We are going to have a large party next Thursday, and music; and the Nepaul General is to honour us with his company. I think I shall die of fright in anticipation of its success, before the day arrives. The amateur singers and performers have been exceedingly kind to me about it, in taking as much trouble as possible off my hands. Can you fancy me acting in the capacity of party giver? This morning I had visits from them to discuss matters connected with it. This evening we attended our Almack's. I enjoyed it rather and danced three sets of quadrilles. The Nepaul General was there looking very beautiful, for he was dressed in his own style with no mixture of English. I cannot say so much of his little boys; one in particular looked for all the world just like the monkeys who go about the streets of London dressed up in uniforms on dogs' backs. Upon this occasion, he wore a scarlet tunic coat, a sword quite as big as himself, and a huge cocked hat and feather just like the one my father wears and which in point of size would have just fitted him also. He was extinguished in it, which was just as well for he is hideous, with an abominable squint owing to his

having poked a sharp instrument into his eye. The
General is actually learning to dance and is much puzzled
by the waltz. He says it makes him so giddy! His troops
have returned to Nepaul. He remains a fortnight or three
weeks longer. I am so ashamed of the length of this; I
must bring it to a close. How much I should like to
know, my dear Mrs Chaplin, whether so much trash
bores you to death; but as I cannot under three months,
or more, I shall e'en take my chance and swim on. I hope
you are all well, as we are at present, my father and all of
us, excepting that old beast Major Macan;★ but he
continues better. Give my most affectionate love to dear
Mrs Fane when you next go to Fulbeck or she goes to
you. I hope her health is as good as when I left her. Love
also, and sincere love, to your good and kind husband
and the same to any to whom it may prove acceptable;
and believe me to remain, my dear Mrs Chaplin, ever
yours

Very affectionately,

I. Fane.

The Governor-General is daily expected but not yet
arrived. A ship called the *Zenobia* is in the river and we
are most anxiously looking for letters, for it is indeed
ages since we have had any. The *Zenobia* has brought us
heaps of letters. Many thanks for a delightful packet
from you dated September 8th 1835.

★ Major Turner Macan, Persian Interpreter to the Commander-in-
Chief. Persian was the Mughal court language and the language of
diplomacy throughout India.

II

February 4th   Today was my day of great anxiety and fuss, being the one on which I made my debut as manager of a large evening party. It had disturbed my rest for many a night, for fear of its turning out a failure. We have but one professional person here worth listening to, Mrs Goodall Atkinson, and we engaged her for our *soirée musicale*; the rest were all amateurs who are in the constant practice of singing in public. They were more good-natured than I can express, and the two principal male performers promised to take all trouble off my hands by arranging the songs and the singers. I met with two direful misfortunes the day it was to take place. A lady who was to accompany her husband in some of his songs was taken sick and could not come; and the person who was to have been the prop and stay of the party was taken so ill that two hours before it began I received a note from him to say that he could not come either. Cannot you fancy how my spirits must have sunk within me at this melancholy event? However, notwithstanding, it went off I think very well. All parties here are duller than dull, but I should say this appeared less so than the generality. We had plenty of singing and about 160 listeners; amongst them the Governor-General and suite and the Nepaul General and suite. The latter was exceedingly amused and happy and made many shrewd and droll remarks. He fell into the hands of Mr James Prinsep, who exercised what he considers his wit upon him to what *I* should consider a provoking degree. For his own amusement he told him things which were not true in answer to questions which he put, which is well enough for those who have the power to discriminate, but in my opinion it is a shame to act so towards those who cannot, and who wish to learn.

Saturday 6th   Major Macan is again very ill, a close prisoner to his room. Christine and I paid him a visit and found him with his wretched pox-marked face scarlet with fever and his hands burning; but he said he was better. Mrs Thoby paid us a long visit on our return. She is charming well again, and beginning to make a slight display of her situation! Poor old Thoby is at the Sandheads.

Monday 8th   There was a large man party this evening, so we females dined over the way with Mrs Beresford, where we were sadly bit by the musquitoes and were all *so* sleepy long before we ought to have been. This is the worst effect of the climate upon us; almost immediately after dinner the lassitude that comes on is very painful, and it is hardly possible to sit up until ten o'clock, the time fixed for going to bed.

Wednesday 10th   I was made very unhappy this morning by lots of morning visitors, all new people whom I had never seen before. Is it not surprising, notwithstanding our having been here for so long now, that we should not yet have done with strange faces? Our party has had the melancholy effect of calling many from their retreats, in hopes I suppose of taking their turn should there be another. I ought to have begun the details of this day by saying I got up this morning at six o'clock, before daylight, to ride. The evenings now are too hot for this exercise, but the mornings until half-past seven are delicious – plenty of wind blowing from the south; but unfortunately this is the wind that blows up the broiling weather. Mrs Beresford and I, John and Captain Campbell ended the day with the play. We saw *Catherine and Petrucio* [an adaptation of Shakespeare's *The Taming of the Shrew*] acted, and exceedingly well acted, and *La Fôret Noire* [possibly *La Fôret Perilleuse* by Tréogaste] which I did not like. There was far too much firing in it to give me any satisfaction. The house was very full of nabobies, and was very hot. The Nepaul General was there, who liked the *moral* of *The Taming of the Shrew*, he said, very much. Perhaps for the future he will act upon it, instead of chopping off heads, which I suppose is what he now does.

Thursday 11th   My father and staff went today to see an iron foundry where they cast great guns, a short distance from hence on the bank of the river. The Nepaul General went and was much pleased, particularly with the boring part of the operation of gun making. In his country it takes three months to do what in this foundry was done in as many minutes, and I dare say the machinery there was very imperfect compared to the same in Europe. This evening we had a dinner party. Mrs Thoby one. Nasty creature, she provoked me more than ever with her detestable ways and proceedings.

Monday 15th   This evening was the reunion ball, to which I had resolved not to go on account of odious Mrs Prinsep. However, Christine persuaded me that so far from staying at home on her account I ought to go, and accordingly I did, but never was more unhappy or annoyed in my lifetime. The *brute's* conduct (you must recollect her poor old man is away sick at the Sandheads) was so bad. If you could but form an idea of the weak silly thing she is!

Thursday 18th   This morning the Nepaul General came to take leave of my father, previous to his departure for Nepaul. In the evening, as Christine, Mrs Beresford and I were driving out, we met him, and just fancy how exceedingly polished and well-bred a man he must be, for he instantly pulled up alongside our carriage for the purpose of wishing us goodbye through his interpreter, hoping to see us as we went up the country. He says he will come 150 miles to meet my father, if he knows when he is passing within that distance of him. We shook hands, made little speeches; and he was so delightfully perfumed with sandalwood that my glove smelt for a long time afterwards. He was magnificently drest in tiger skin, and as he imitates my father as much as he can, he had hung upon his breast a silver something like my father's orders, suspended by a sky blue ribbon. The other night at Mrs Plowden's party he wore a general officer's (I believe) uniform coat, with a large cocked hat and plume of feathers such as my father wears. In the course of the evening he took it off and displayed his oddly shaven and shorn head.

Sunday 21st   I think I told you in a previous piece of journal that we were all in a small way trying our luck in the lottery. We had amongst us three numbers to share, as we hoped; but in spite of favourable dreams etc., etc., this morning at one fell swoop our hopes were destroyed, both our remaining numbers having turned up blanks. Whilst we were at Barrackpore our first had taken the same line, so now I shall not try again at present.

Tuesday 23rd   This evening we had a large dinner party, both lady and gentleman, and a pretty scrape we have all got into. We thought Mrs Thoby Prinsep was the lady for my father to take into dinner, instead of which there were *two* who ought to have gone before her. You may suppose my feelings towards Mrs Thoby. Nothing but stupid ignorance would have led me to commit this *faux pas*. Unfortunately the injured lady they tell me is a great stickler about her rights, and is very likely to take it amiss. I must do Mrs Thoby the justice to say she was very uncomfortable at the mistake, and also that she behaved herself all the evening with more propriety than usual. Her husband has returned and I am more at my ease, *much*, in consequence. He is quite well again, but has much flesh to pick up. In consequence of this error of etiquette we thought the party would have spent the night with us, for you may remember my telling you that no one can stir to go home here until *the* lady of the party makes the move; and as poor Mrs Thoby had, contrary to her wishes, become the great lady for the night, the *right* one did not choose to stir; and as she again did not wish to extend further her usurped rights, nothing would induce *her* to stir either. I am in the act of reading Mrs Buller's journal, and I am thinking of requesting you to *save* these *entertaining* sheets I send you, that I may publish them on my return to England! I must say I think hers contains quite as much nonsense as mine, but then I must add there are bursts of good writing interspersed with sensible remarks, which, alas! mine cannot boast of.

Thursday 25th   We all went to the play this evening to see *Macbeth*. It was exceedingly well got up. The witch scene was very well managed, but the hags themselves not well drest, that is to say they were too well drest, and would have been much better had they been less smart. Mr Holroyd was one, and Mr James Prinsep another. Our little milliner acted Lady Macbeth, and really in a most extraordinary manner. She has not either figure or voice to make this character what it ought to be, which is no fault of hers; but for those who had not seen Mrs Siddons in the same character, Mrs Leach appeared wonderful. Nasty Mrs Thoby was of our party, and did not behave with what I should call propriety. She has a sister, a Miss Pattle, a little, ugly, underbred-looking thing; but she has the reputation of being very clever, which is better than beauty.* She is courted by one Captain Smyth, an A.D.C. of Sir C. Metcalfe's. These two doves sat behind me at the play, and the tiresome creatures did nothing but coo the whole time. I wished them at Jericho, for when I go to a play I like to listen to the whole of it, and they kept up such an incessant jabber that they disturbed me much. Sir C. Metcalfe is finishing his reign in a most unsatisfactory manner, in consequence of allowing his failing of favouritism to far and far outstep justice. He has bestowed a situation on his secretary (a young man who has no other claim than that of being much liked by Sir Charles), which has put the Calcutta world into a hurly burly and has given the newspapers a fine topic for discussion. There is also an A.D.C., a boy of nineteen, without a scrap of beard, whom he has also favoured in a manner which if he had *not* done would have been quite as much to his credit. I believe he returns to England immediately. I wonder how the climate will agree with him. He leads the most singular life here. He never stirs out of the house excepting to go

---

* Julia Margaret Pattle (1815–79), later Mrs Cameron, the famous photographer. See Biographical Notes, p. 33.

every Thursday to Barrackpore by water, and to return to Calcutta by ten o'clock on Monday morning, in time for Council. He never takes the least exercise, further than a few paces in his verandah, eats like an elephant, and drinks nothing but champagne – and plenty of that.

Wednesday March 9th   I am so dreadfully in arrears with my journal and have so much to tell you, I don't know how to begin. We have been daily expecting the arrival of the Governor-General [Lord Auckland] for some time past. On Friday last, the 4th of March, he landed at eleven o'clock at night, without honour or compliment. He had been telegraphed in the morning as being in the river, and two steamers went down to tow him up. He was expected to land at about five o'clock, and the troops were out and ready to receive him, forming a passage from the landing place up to Government House. It was to have been a pretty sight; the *Jupiter* would have manned its arms, and all sorts of nice things happen. The Captain contrived to stick him in the mud, so he and his people were obliged to get into the steamer and come up to Calcutta in that, which occasioned so much delay that he did not arrive until the late hour I have mentioned. My father and his staff went to Government House at a little after four, and had to wait there until after his arrival. They did not sit down to dinner until nine o'clock, nor get away till late. The troops were dismissed at nine, so he sneaked into his seat of government as he had previously done into the Cape and Rio, where he had touched.

The next day we ladies were appointed to go in our evening drive to call upon the Misses Eden, but in consequence of a misunderstanding about the hour we did not see them. You may suppose how grieved we were at this. However, we had to go again the following morning, and then we were more fortunate. We got on famously. They are both great talkers, both old, both ugly, and both s---k like polecats! Sir H. Chamberlain informed some of our young gentlemen that on board ship they were so dreadful in this respect that those who were so lucky as to sit next to them at dinner had their appetites much interfered with. I think if they go on as well as they have begun we shall have reason to be satisfied with the head of our society. At least they are a very pleasing contrast to vulgar Lady Ryan, our present head. As soon as we found them actually safe ashore we determined we would have a ball, so as Mrs Thoby Prinsep had cards out for one we resolved, as we dislike her so much, to do a bit of spite (which was amiable enough on the part of Christine and myself), and not allow her to have the first of the new arrivals. We only determined to have the ball on Friday, and fixed the following Tuesday for the day it should be given. In England this would not have answered, but here things are done differently. Our house is perfect for an entertainment of the sort, for our dining room is immense. This we made the ballroom, and we had reared at one end of it a nice platform for the musicians. My father desired the use of the band of the 44th Regiment, which we placed in our magnificent verandah to play between whiles; and although it is a shocking band, it had a generally good effect. We had the Governor-General and suite, and the ex-Governor-General and suite, besides all Calcutta. We were well satisfied with it, though I have no doubt plenty of ill-natured things are said on the subject. It was kept up with seemingly much spirit until two o'clock, which is a late hour for this climate. The next day, Wednesday 9th, we had a huge dinner party for Lord Auckland and the heads of Government here. We sat down thirty in number, and I was placed between the reigning and the ex-Governors. I would rather have been between two more insignificant personages, but still I am getting bolder I suppose, for I did not feel so frightened as I did when I sat next to Sir C. Metcalfe on a former occasion.

Thursday 10th   We went this morning to pay some visits, but it was so dreadfully hot we could not do all we intended. The hot weather is now fairly set in. The thermometer is about 80 in the room when the punkah is not going, but it will be higher than this I believe. During the heat it is the custom here to shut up every window and only allow sufficient light to be able just to see. This is considered coolness, and so I really believe it is; but new arrivals like us find it difficult to persuade ourselves of the truth of the system. Today I have adopted it for the first time, and with the glass before me at 80, and the punkah going at a great rate, I am as cool as a cucumber. Mrs Thoby Prinsep's ball was tonight, to which we all went save John. I was so tired and footsore from all I had danced at my own ball that I would much rather have gone to bed; so I would not dance, only staid one hour and was at home and in bed by eleven o'clock. The hostess as usual acted like a fool, but what can you expect of a pig, but a grunt!

Sunday 13th   I did not go to church this morning, it was such a hot day; but by shutting up every part of the house you cannot imagine how cool it feels. About half past five o'clock in the afternoon I went into the verandah with John, and I do assure you it was exactly like entering the mouth of an oven. John threw down a wine-glass of cold water on the floor of the verandah, and before you could crack your fingers every drop of it was dried up, just as water does when poured on hot iron; and yet none of us indoors was the least bit uncomfortable. Mrs Beresford complains dreadfully, but then she is of so restless a disposition she has no chance of being cool.

Monday 14th   At a little before ten this morning we were all dressed in our best to go with my father to Government House to witness the ceremony of investing Sir C. Metcalfe with the star and ribbon of the Knight's Grand Cross. The room appointed for the ceremony was the ballroom, and it was as full as ever it could hold of ladies and gentleman, military and civil, and natives. A fine chair, stool and piece of carpet were placed at one end of the immense room for Lord Auckland. Sir C. Metcalfe was to come in at the opposite end supported by my father and Sir Jeremiah Dickson, who is a small knight of some sort. He was placed right before Lord Auckland, who in a frightful state of nervous excitement made a long and complimentary speech, the perspiration, from fright and heat, streaming well down his face. But he acquitted himself very well, all things considered. Then Sir C. replied, suffering much at first from agitation, which was quite natural; but he made an exceedingly neat, tidy speech, without saying too much or too little. He and my father then *backed* all the way down the room again and so ended the ceremony, which was, I assure you, quite touching, even to the spectators. The Misses Eden looked very ugly, but were affable and amiable to a degree. In the evening there was a grand ball and supper in honour of the occasion, which was well attended. We did not stay for the supper and were home by twelve o'clock.

Tuesday 15th   Nothing but visitors during the morning. We went to the play this evening, and in consequence of the arrival of the Governor-General we have tumbled down in the world and are turned out of our comfortable place into a much less comfortable one. It had this advantage, that Mrs Thoby could not join us, and I had the satisfaction of seeing her a mile off, looking very disconsolate for want of her *old* flirt, as well as the pleasure of seeing her make an early departure because, no doubt, she was bored. The play was *William Tell* [by James Sheridan Knowles], which was tedious, and the after-piece *Old and Young*. It lasted altogether too long. It was hot and the house smelt bad of perspirationy people; and the musquitoes were intolerable. I wish you could see what a snug little house I have established in my room to defend myself by day from these pests. It is a little room–shade of musquito gauze, which just holds my writing table, chair and couch, and the punkah hangs just over it. I look like a bird in a cage. If you could but see the melancholy condition of my legs and feet even now, though I have been six months in India; but as they do not come to regular sores, as they did three months ago, they are by comparison nothing.

Wednesday 16th   Last night there was a concert at Government House, which, as a point of duty, I went to, but quite against my inclination, for in this warm climate to be out three nights successively is too much. The eldest Miss Eden [Emily] is laid up already with fever, but she was much better that night and not likely to die. They have arrived at a most unfortunate season. I think Lord Auckland's manners and appearance are particularly against his holding so high a situation. He seems so painfully shy and frightened. I sat next to Miss F. Eden at the concert, and talked to her, and liked her very much. The music here, from the professional people, one never thinks of listening to, it is so bad. Mr

Melville* dined with us. He comes whenever he likes, poor old figure, and has great argumentations, which he seems to delight in.

Thursday 17th   Nothing occurred very particular today, excepting Christine's baby was vaccinated and roared frightfully on the occasion, I understand; but I was not present. The pus was taken from the arm of a black child. If he does not turn out most particularly dark it will be very odd, having been nursed for the first two weeks after his birth by a black woman and now having the vaccine dirt from the constitution of a black child. At present he is exceedingly fair, and I believe he is still pretty, but he is drest such an object that no child of four months old could look well. At that age, in my opinion, they require aid from cap and frock. The weather now is so hot that infants go about all but naked, so he wears nothing but a thin cambric muslin frock without a bit of even *short* sleeve, a piece of flannel twisted round his body, and no cap – and he has not a scrap of hair. From this description I think you will allow that *his* are trying circumstances. Miss Eden is out again, which information will I am sure give you great satisfaction!

Saturday 19th   Fancy my being again crippled with musquito bites! I have a place on my leg which I have over-scratched, nearly a quarter of a yard long. I am most unfortunate. They are much more venomous and numerous now than they were in the cold weather. I am afraid I have swelled this journal to too great a length, so I must bring it to a conclusion. Don't swear

---

* Philip Melville, Secretary to Government in the Military Department.

at its folly. Distribute my love right and left to all friends, and a large portion at Fulbeck. I hope and trust that Mrs Fane is quite well; tell her I often think and talk of her. Believe me, my dear Mrs Chaplin,

Very affectionately yours,

I. Fane.

It is decided that Sir C. Metcalfe remains here as Lieutenant-Governor of Agra.

III

March 21st 1836   This morning I despatched a large
bundle of journal to you and in the afternoon at half past
five o'clock Mrs Beresford and I started in the most
unpromising weather for a place called Tittaghur
[Titagarh], about fourteen miles from Calcutta, where
she had a house lent her for change of air for her child,
who has not been quite well. She invited me to go and
stay with her. This would be a very nice house if it was in
repair; but it is very much otherwise, and looks
swarming with big spiders, large ants and all sorts of
varmint. It is close on the banks of the Hooghly and
decidedly much cooler than Calcutta, and as our
residence, or at least mine, is very temporary, the
rubbishy house is of no consequence. I have brought
with me only three men and two maids, so unless upon
the English principle 'too many cooks' etc., etc., I shall
be *very* comfortable for *three* days. Barrackpore is about
one mile from us, so last night Marc drove me in the park
and we went to see the elephants drink. We were too late
to see them fed. I have the happiness of being completely
laid up, with *both* my legs disabled again from the
tormenting musquitoes. If dear Mrs Fane of Wimpole
St. did but know it how nasty she would think me!

Monday 27th   This morning at six o'clock I left
Tittaghur for home. I spent a very comfortable quiet

week with my legs on the sofa all the morning, plaistered and bandaged, and in the evening I drove out with Mrs Beresford. The park at Barrackpore is delightful for this purpose, and open to the public. There is an avenue which extends for fourteen miles, which is the direct road from Calcutta to Barrackpore, and which is very nice to drive upon. The evening before we left Miss Eden sent us an elephant to ride, but I did not particularly enjoy it. It hurt my bad legs so much, and it was a very rough elephant. Mrs Beresford read *The Admiral's Daughter* [unidentified] and *The Deformed* [*The Deformed Transformed*, by Byron] to me. At the first I cried buckets full, although it is so unnatural a tale; and the other I liked very much, but it did not make me cry. We had whilst there a storm known here by the name of a norwester. It brings lots of wind from that quarter and with it violent rain, thunder and lightning to match. These occur very often during the hot weather and are a great luxury, as they cool the air beautifully for a day or two. All the people excepting myself dined at Government House. I did not on account of my legs.

Friday 31st   Today all the party with the exception of Christine and myself went to Barrackpore. We were of course invited also, but *I* could not go on account of my legs. I cannot get on shoes or stockings. Christine could not go on account of the baby, so she and I are left in quiet possession of this great big house. I quite rejoice my legs are bad, for I find Mrs Thoby Prinsep is there, and I dislike her so much she would have destroyed any comfort I might otherwise have had. I am so amused when I reflect upon the different accounts you probably hear of this same individual. Caroline writes to Louisa, I have not the least doubt, in an ecstasy about her, for they are like two fond lovers. Carry writes to her always "My darling Sarah", besides lots of other folly, such as "I always told you you were perfection", etc., etc., for she does not at all see she is either an idiot or a scandalous flirt. How different is my account.

On Friday evening in our drive Christine and I met a native wedding party. The bridegroom looked about *ten* years old, and was riding a pony. He must have been someone of consequence, there was so grand a procession; but alas! we had no one with us to tell us anything, and although we tried to make out from the servants who were with us about it, it was of no use for, as you may suppose, we are too imperfect in the language to go beyond asking for what we want, and as for understanding what they say, it is quite out of the question. The bride of course did not shew. I dare say she was about six years old!

Monday April 4th   My father returned from Barrackpore having spent a most agreeable time of course, as he was in such charming society! He went to the play in the evening. I did not, my legs and feet are so bad. I have got *seven* sore places on one, and *four* on the other, all from musquitoes. I ought to have told you that on Saturday Sir Charles Metcalfe left this on his way to his new seat of government, *viz* Agra, to which place he is appointed Governor. Captain Higgenson, to whom he gave the situation which gave so much offence, has thrown it up in order to follow the fortunes of his master, and has taken instead the office of private secretary to Sir C.M., as well as A.D.C., but still I believe the two combined are not equivalent to the one he has given up, so he is extolled for his disinterestedness. 'It is an ill wind' etc., etc., for Lord Auckland has given our friend Mr Melville Mr Higgenson's thrown-up situation, which is the same he held when in India before, but the salary is not so good as it was then. It is rather odd that John said to Mr Melville one day before it was actually offered to him: 'How should you like the situation?'; to which Mr Melville replied: 'What, take Mr Higgenson's leavings!' However, he has, and I hope he will soon make his fortune therein.

April 12th   I have been obliged to pause in my journal for many days. My eyes are so bad, and I have nothing to relate in consequence of my close confinement. I thought I might as well take advantage of it to give them a rest. If you hear any complaining of me as a correspondent, will you defend me on the score of my eyes? I do assure you it is no idle excuse, but I find it *more*, much, than my eyes can manage to write my daily bit to you.

On Sunday April 10th began a celebrated Hindoo festival called the Churrack Pooga [*carkh puja*, 'wheel ceremony', an expiatory rite]. No doubt you have read of it in histories of India. It lasts for three days altogether and on the first takes place the ceremony of the unfortunate creatures sticking sharp instruments into various parts of their persons. None but quite the lowest castes undergo these tortures, who are *paid*, I am told, about four annas, that is, about 6d, by those of higher caste to do it for them. They fortify themselves well for what they are to endure by the use of opium and ardent spirits, and are satisfied with their small pay as well as the veneration with which they are regarded by their friends. *I* have a very enquiring mind, or else if you please, a large share of curiosity, and have in consequence no idea of coming so far without seeing all that is to be seen; so upon finding at half-past seven in the morning that John was going out in his buggy to see the fun, I turned out of bed, slipped on my dressing gown, a bonnet and shawl, and unwashed, bad legs and all,

72

was carried down, put into his vehicle, and off we set together. The crowd was something quite indescribable; but we saw processions of these poor deluded wretches, some with a long iron rod, about six or seven feet in length and the thickness of my little finger, run right through their tongues and, notwithstanding, hopping and skipping. Others had six or seven of these stuck at once into their bodies. I saw one man with a great hole made in his arm and a *live* snake drawn through it! I began to be very disgusted and had I staid much longer John would have brought me home in a faint. The heat was dreadful, and although I had nothing on but my nightgown and dressing ditto I was sopping with pers.

The following day was to be the swinging by hooks in the back, which I know *you* have heard of in England, because *I* have. Although I felt ashamed of my unfeminine curiosity, this exhibition I was resolved not to miss, so I put on an old poke bonnet and a veil and off I set in a gig with Marc Beresford at five o'clock in the evening. We got a capital situation close to the scene of action and I had the satisfaction of seeing two men perform as follows. A very high bamboo is stuck into the ground, and at the very tip top of this another is placed horizontally. At each end are ropes. To one, the man is suspended; the other a man holds and twists him round with. Two large hooks are run through a large muscle which I am told is to be found under the shoulder blades, one under each, and then the ropes are fastened to these. The unfortunate man has a band round him besides, so that his *whole* weight does not rest on the hooks, but the very circumstance of their being in his body at all is sufficiently horrid. He swings round very fast for about ten minutes, kicking his legs about and performing antics in the air. He also takes up with him fruit etc., which he tastes and then throws down to the population below. Marc went close to the man and saw him unhooked. Not a drop of blood flows from the places, and as soon as the hooks are withdrawn the man throws himself on the ground and a friend presses the places with his feet; a cloth is then tied over them, and I myself saw the man trip away just as if nothing had happened. It is not nearly so disgusting a sight as the one the day before. Indeed, one man did not appear to suffer at all. The other did, for he caught hold of the rope above him as if to ease himself. Poor benighted creatures, what a pity it is that they cannot understand that such tortures are quite needless. I met no European, so saw the sight safely and well.

Tuesday 12th   The Miss Edens have an at home every alternate Tuesday, so last night all our party went, excepting me and my legs. Fancy how good-natured the people are here. They say of me that I have nothing the matter with me, but I like lying on my couch and so pretend I am bad! The brutes. I wish those that say so had all my bad places on the tips of their noses. The Misses Eden are very amiable to me and are doing their utmost to become intimate; but the hot sun and my calamities prevent much yet. When I mend I dare say we shall get on.

Saturday 16th   One of the *very few* nice, lady-like people of this place paid us a morning visit, Lady D'Oyly by name. She has a cousin who lives with her who goes by the name of the *alligator*. She is six feet high, thinner and *flatter* than I am, with an astonishingly short waist. She looks about forty, is unmarried, and *dances* and *waltzes* at all the balls!!! She seems an amiable, excellent creature and I like her very much. My father was a little ailing today; but nothing much amiss, and I think it was only in consequence of drinking too much

74

champagne the day before. John was also what he calls *seedy*.

Sunday 17th   My father well, John more *seedy*. Mrs Holroyd drove out with us, and the Beresfords and Mr Melville dined with us and so ended our day. By the bye, I put my legs to the ground for the first time in three weeks, although I have yet three wounds not quite healed. The heat is monstrous: 93 in the *shade*, 83 in the shut-up and punkahed rooms; but it is to be worse next month.

Tuesday 19th   John not at all well, but his sickness is nothing of the least consequence. It is a slight attack of fever, which the doctor says would have been bad if he had not taken it in time. We had a large dinner party this evening, with the Governor-General, but not the ladies of the family. They do not mean to go anywhere. They find it too great an exertion during the hot season, and their home entertainments quite enough. The climate does not seem very suitable to the eldest. She is for the second time confined to her bed with headache and fever. Lord Auckland appears a very good-natured unaffected man, but so distressingly shy and nervous. I have found no whisperings of faction, so I suppose as yet he gives satisfaction; but these are early times. By the bye, he appointed the surgeon of the *Jupiter* as his surgeon, which has not pleased. I did not dine at table on account of my legs, as I am forbid to eat; but I appeared in the evening and we had some nice singing. Mrs Thoby of course of the party. Nasty fool!

Thursday 21st   The Misses Eden have pressed me much to pay them a visit at Barrackpore, so today I came. There is not a soul staying, besides the household, but myself. They are the most good-natured, unaffected creatures I ever saw, and one cannot feel afraid of any of them. Miss Eden is sick, and I should doubt whether this climate will agree with her.

Friday 22nd   Passed a sufficiently agreeable day in the society of the lady governesses general. I begin to think my own house is the only place for me now that my eyes are become so unserviceable. I cannot read, write, work, draw or do anything to amuse myself, so I find time tedious. At home one can potter about. Besides, I have found a young girl who comes daily to read to me for an hour or two in Calcutta. She reads astonishingly well and no word, hardly, puzzles her; but the monotony of her tone is indescribable. However, it is better than no reading at all. It does amuse me and put me to sleep sometimes, and I flatter myself she may improve from practice in her intonation. She is fourteen, has been married some months, and gets eight rupees per month, i.e. 16/- of our money, for this her wonderful feat. I drove out with Miss Eden alone and we went to see a leopard and hyena, which had arrived in the morning for the menagerie. The wild beasts had been done away with in Lord W. Bentinck's time on account of the expense; but these folk are going to have a few, as well as birds, and I expect they will be hauled over the coals for it – at least by the newspaper writers. A ship is going to sail so I must despatch this. My best love to all friends, and with the sincere hope this may find all well, believe me, my dear Mrs Chaplin,

Very affectionately yours,

I. Fane.

IV

April 27th   Today I returned to Calcutta after a week's residence at Barrackpore. Lord Auckland and his youngest sister and suite returned to town as usual on Monday last to fulfil their respective duties; but Miss Eden, who has had fever and has been otherwise ill, stayed on here to recruit, and she requested me to keep her company, which I have been doing. Today, Thursday, they all came down again, so I take my departure, although they all intended I should remain until they go back again next Monday. But I feel I have said my say for the present and am also afraid of out-staying my welcome. Miss Eden is a very particularly nice person, so sensible, clever, well-informed, religious and good in every possible way, and I have enjoyed my solitariness with her more than a shy person, and one who always has the impression on her mind that she is neither sensible nor agreeable, could possibly expect to do.* But these feelings you will not

* It is sad to have to record that the esteem was not, apparently, reciprocated. Her sister, Mrs Lister, asked Emily Eden: 'Do you find amongst your European acquaintances any pleasing or accomplished women?' Emily replied: 'Not one – not the sixth part of one; there is not anybody I can prefer to any other body, if I think of sending to ask one to come and pay me a visit, or to go out in the carriage; and when we have had any of them for two or three days at Barrackpore, there is a *morne* feeling at the end of their visit that it will be tiresome when it comes round to their turn of coming again. I really believe the climate

77

understand, because you won't believe I possess them!

My residence here has been of great use to me. My wounds are all but healed, and as there is an entire absence of my tormentors here I have no fresh bites. I expect they will make up for this and look upon me after my week's absence as a fresh importation and act accordingly. The evenings are so much cooler at Barrackpore than at Calcutta. One's drive really seems to do one good, whereas in the other place it only serves to kill time. The nights also, I dare say, would have been the same, if I could have taken advantage of all the doors and windows my room possessed; but one I could not open because it led into Lord Auckland's sanctum, and another I could not open because my *six* black attendants slept on the other side of it. So I could not make a through draft, and unless one can manage this by night the heat is intense and one's sleep much disturbed. I found all well in Calcutta, excepting by the bye poor John, who is gone on a cruise for a few days' change of air. His liver is affected already and he has a bad cough. My father says if he is not better on his return he will send him back to England directly. I must say he has to thank himself for his present state. He has been so very incautious, and because in Jamaica he did things with impunity fancied he might do the same here, although warned to the contrary.

Saturday 29th   John returned from his cruise today very much benefitted. He has completely lost his voice, but this proceeds only from a relaxed throat. He has lost

---

is to blame.' [*Miss Eden's Letters*, edited by Violet Dickinson, p.280]. But it is just possible that she had in mind only the ladies then present in Calcutta. If so, Isabella is exempt, because at the time of this letter (January 1837) she was away in the upper provinces.

his cough and all other bad symptoms, and the Dr. says he will do. He says it was so cool down the river that a blanket, if he had had it with him, would have been very comfortable. The very sound of a blanket now in Calcutta makes one start, so frightfully are we all grilling. The thermometer in the room is 84, in the *shade* 96 and God knows what in the sun, but my father thinks it quite pleasant weather! So much for occupation! I must say for women, and *occupied* men, this climate does very well; but for those like the aides-de-camp of this establishment, who have little or nothing to do, it must be anything but agreeable. The whole house is shut up tight from nine in the morning until six in the evening, and in the course of the twenty-four hours *three* hours in all it is possible to spend out of doors.

Monday May 2nd   This day a year ago exactly we sailed from Cowes. Major Macan is so ill again. Another abcess has just broken on his lungs, and he is in an indescribable state of emaciation and weakness. He will not, if alive, go up the country with us. He will in many respects be a great loss to my father. He is very useful, but so detestable a character I never beheld, nor so unpopular a man. It is wicked how I hate him, and yet I have reason to do so, for I know all his ingratitude to my father and all his hateful ways. It provokes me beyond bearing to think that it is best my father should be deceived by him.

Tuesday 3rd   A great dinner at Babington Macaulay's to the Governor-General. Very long and very tedious. The weather is much too hot now to stir from home. We were 35. The Misses Eden have the best of it for they go nowhere, only entertain at home.

Saturday 7th   Nothing the least worth putting on paper has occurred since I last scribbled on this, for we have done nothing but have one middle-sized dinner party and perspire from morning till night and from night till morning. My father even finds it hot and goes without his waistcoat or stock and with his gills turned down *en garçon*. Our riding horses have started for Allahabad, which looks like business, and we are full of preparations for up the country, although we do not start ourselves until September.

May 12th   I have nothing to put down excepting we are very hot, but all quite well. John has quite recovered. The mangoe fish is in season, which is reckoned the best fish in Calcutta, and that is not saying very much in its praise either, for we are miserably off in this respect. The mangoe fruit is also in season (the fish and fruit are always in season together) and those that like it at all like it very much. There is no medium. It is decidedly not the best fruit we have tasted, but then we are much prejudiced in favour of peaches, nectarines, cherries, gooseberries, raspberries and a much longer list of European fruits. The mangoe fruit when *iced* is super excellent, a luxury we can indulge in although the thermometer stands at 83 the minimum. We have a regular supply of ice from America, and an excellent ice-house built by subscription. We have a species of Grange to whose shop we go of an afternoon. The ices fall far short of hers in my opinion, but a *middling* ice in this climate is better than none at all.

Monday 16th   We dined this evening at Government House, the first time we have been gay for ages. In the morning we had been studying the book of precedence appertaining to the rank and quality of this city as laid down by the King in Council. We were laughing and joking about this and each settling how we stood. It was arranged that *I* was nobody at all and need never trouble myself as to when and where I was to be in any grand march or at any great dinner. I was perfectly satisfied with the decision of the court, for provided that I get in quietly and snugly it is little matter to me whether I am first or twentieth. Conceive then my horror and amazement when Lord Auckland stepped forward upon this occasion and walked me out under his wing before *three* other *married* ladies, one of whom I am told is a great stickler at etiquette. It was totally wrong, but still as I was as innocent as the new babe of the misdemeanour I hope and trust my character may be spared. It was upon the whole a pleasant dinner. In the evening I talked a good deal to Miss Eden, in whom I delight. We were home by ten minutes past ten. Mrs Thoby Prinsep was of the party and did not sit next to my father. She looked stupefied and bored to death. She told Marc Beresford after dinner it was sentiment made her look so die-away. Mrs James Prinsep had been confined the morning before of her first child, and that day it was in a dying state. So Mrs Thoby got up this sorrowful countenance on the occasion. I am very sorry for the poor parents; to lose a first child is so very melancholy. She is a quiet little empty-headed woman, but then *he* is certainly not the first and, report says, not the second either.

Tuesday 17th   Major Macan made his appearance upstairs again at breakfast this morning, after an absence of many weeks. He was carried upstairs and helped across the room. He is thinner than before his disappearance, which God knows was unnecessary, but in face he did not look a bit worse than previous to his last attack. The next must be his last I should think, wretched man. There are constantly during the hot weather here great fires which destroy at 'one fell swoop' numbers of the poor natives' huts, which indeed is not to be wondered at, considering the very combustible material of which they are built – *viz* mat and bamboo. There was a terrific one this night a very little way from hence, which we went to the very tip top of the house to see. We had a magnificent view of it. Our dobie [*dhobi*] or washerman lived in the direction of it and for some time we trembled for our clothes. In this puggy country, let me tell you, the once-weekly wash is no joke, even for one individual. As this good man has the washing of the whole house had he been burnt out the losses would have been considerable. But he was not one of the sufferers.

June 3rd　　My journal has come to a sad standstill, but when I tell you I have been ill you will not blame me for it. About ten days ago I was attacked with fever and a violent sore throat. To remedy the former I was kept in bed and starved and for the latter I had a great blister applied. I was only ill altogether for a week, but considerably pulled down and thinned even by so short an attack. Miss Eden asked me to go to Barrackpore to recruit, which I was only too happy to do, and I came here last Monday, May 30th. Mrs Beresford is also here for the same purpose, and up till yesterday us two, the two Miss Edens, two A.D.C.s and the Doctor formed the whole of our party. Yesterday Lord Auckland arrived, and some more staff and some visitors – two of the nastiest, pertest little people I ever beheld, a Mr and Mrs Cockerell. He is now the principal agent here, and sorry should I be to trust my savings in his hands. She was a Miss Newcoman, the daughter of a First Lord of that name by a drunken cook. She is an odious little satirical thing, bordering on the side of good-looking. I begin to think Miss Fanny Eden somewhat of a bore; she has such immense spirits and laughs so much at nothing at all. She jokes much in the same line, and makes such a fool of herself about Willy Osborne,* the Military Secretary, her nephew. Miss [Emily] Eden I still think charming, and indeed the other is a great acquisition to society, more particularly the society here, which is so dull. I have got some such nice ivory letters made at Moorshedabad, which Mr Melville gave me, and the two last evenings after dinner we have amused ourselves in the most innocent manner with these, giving each other words to make out. The Governor-General amused himself with them also and, I am happy to say, was not particularly brilliant at finding out the given word. Upon which Miss Fanny observed, 'Well, George, I am glad we have found something to puzzle you at last!' So you see, he must be a genius, although the Tories could not find it out.

June 8th   A ship sails tomorrow, I believe, so I must bring this to a conclusion. Distribute my love to all to whom it may be acceptable and believe me, dear Mrs Chaplin,

Yours very affectionately,

I. Fane.

* Lieut. The Hon. W.G. Osborne, Miltary Secretary to the Governor-General. Author of *The Court and Camp of Runjeet Singh*. Emily Eden dedicated *Up the Country* to him.

V

Saturday June 11th   My father received such a magnificent present of fruit from Rajah somebody, upon huge dishes, neatly covered over with pretty little fringed carpets, which I longed to steal. The mangoes were beautiful to look at, but odious to taste. This fruit is falling off very much. Some time ago they were delicious.

Monday 13th   I did a great deal today, for I got up at half-past four o'clock to drive in the break, because (I ought to have mentioned) on Sunday evening was the first sympton, or preparation for, our rainy season. We had a most delicious pour down of rain, such as you *untravelled* people could not form an idea of, and which refreshed the parched ground and made the air delightfully cool. At eleven o'clock Christine and I took advantage of this to go and pay a part out of our immense list of visits, which had been due for a long time. In the afternoon we took another drive, contrary to our expectation, for the clouds looked so threatening; and we ended the day with a dinner party of eighteen, and not at all an agreeable one. The people were dull and vulgar for the most part.

Tuesday 14th   Another dinner party today. The Governor-General dined with us, and the Misses Eden very good-naturedly broke their rule of dining nowhere in Calcutta out of consideration of our speedy departure, in order to see as much of us as they can, which is particularly amiable and civil of them. Lord A., my father and two others played at whist (it is quite a novelty to see anything done in this country of an evening) and His Lordship won a rupee, i.e., 2 shillings and 3d English money! Just consider how very provoking: just as the company began to arrive such packets of letters were brought to my father from England and we had to wait until the next morning in expectation. Upon opening my eyes at six o'clock though, they were feasted with your most interesting journal dated February 9th. It is a great relief to my mind, your having begun to receive mine. Now my only fear is you will receive too many and too much, and you will be bored to death with the trumpery I write you. In spite of the calamity which befell me about Dinah, I am going to try my luck with a European maid. There is a very nice widow here, just come out from England, who has one child at home and whose whole thoughts are centred in this child. She lived in this country for some years some time back. I got a darling old ayah in the place of Dinah, who has lived with me up to this time, but as she could not, on account of her health, go up the country with me, I have parted with her now. She recommended me another, who could, but she is so horridly stupid and blind I cannot stand her. My other old woman made nine shots at one hook and eye unsuccessfully; this one makes *thirteen*, and as I think in such a case I should certainly be left behind on the march, I am tempted, by what I hear of this individual, to try her.

June 21st   This morning, when my father went to Council, which is held at Government House, I took my work and went with him to sit with the Miss Edens. The eldest, who draws so beautifully, promised to take our Jemidar [*jamadar*, a native army officer] for my album, so I went to chaperon him. I don't know whether the poor man's feelings were those of pleasure or pain, but he looked very queer. He is such a nice man, and my great *affection* for him led me to wish to have his likeness. Time slipped away very pleasantly in their society. The heat going and coming was dreadful. The rains ought to be here by this time but although it looks very threatening they won't pour down.

Tuesday 22nd   We dined this evening with one of the members of Council, by name Shakespeare. If you could but see Mrs! She has got eleven children, looks ninety and you would not know her from a corpse. Yet she is about another. The Governor-General and Misses Eden dined there. In my struggle to get to the cool side of the room I got next to Lord Auckland, to my disgust. I am sick of him, for in consequence of being a somebody here it so often falls to my lot to find myself by his side. However, I had his frisky secretary on my other, who talked much to me, and the dinner was pleasant. When eleven o'clock came I was surprised.

Thursday 23rd   We had a friendly society to dinner at home today. Mr and Mrs Prinsep, and Mr Holroyd. Mrs H. was to have been of the party, but had a stiff neck and could not come. Mrs Thoby is better in favour with me just now; she has been behaving herself very quietly for some time past. Her folly one can easily forgive, and her good nature, or rather her obliging qualities, cover this sin.

Saturday 25th   I went this morning to see Mrs Beresford for the first time since her illness. She was in bed. I do not know what to make of her malady. I know I wish she was safe in England, and I am in great hopes (for Marc's sake) it will not be long ere she is. He is actually worn out from all the fatigue he has undergone on her account, and today actually fell off his chair in a faint brought on by want of rest. We had a large dinner party tonight and some very nice music in the evening, both vocal and instrumental, by amateurs.

Sunday 26th   I went to church and heard our most detestable preacher. John went to sleep and snored. It was very hot at times during the service, which perhaps added to the dreadful performance of the clergyman and was sufficient excuse for John's irregularity of conduct. On my return from church I went to see Mrs Beresford. I do not like this duty, for I know not what to say to her. The rainy season began today, with heavy showers and fine intervals. The evening held up and we all took a delightful ride on horseback into parts of the environs of Calcutta which we had never visited before. Mrs Prinsep lends me her horse, which is more than I deserve after all the abuse I have at different times lavished upon her; but I have been much more civil to her of late, because she has been much more regular in her conduct.

Monday 27th   The King's birthday, kept here by a ball given by the Governor-General. We of course went to it – as a duty, nothing else I assure you. We staid until 12 o'clock and I never was more bored in my life. On our road to the ball we met the Mahratta chief (who has been here for some time and who came for the purpose of asking protection from the Government) proceeding there in state. Such a curious cavalcade; he was borne in a very odd kind of palanquin and a figure preceded him calling out in an audible tone his various titles. I saw him in the ballroom, looking very bored and miserable. His dress was so odd, at least the lower part of it, for he had a kind of trowser which formed trowser and stocking in one, and by these latter fitted him tight – and his legs were just like skewers. It had a very odd effect. No fuss has been made with him, so he is not an interesting character. Miss Eden sent me home my picture of our Jemidar today. She has done it so beautifully, and it is safely established in my album, ready to shew my friends in England and also to recall this interesting man to my recollection when we bid him a final adieu.

It is quite settled. Mrs Beresford returns immediately to England. Wretched woman, she will I expect fret and fume herself just as sick there, without her husband, as she has done here, in consequence of the heat, the absence of her child and a thousand other fancied troubles. She has completely exhausted her poor husband. He is now quite ill from sleepless nights and attendance upon her night and day, added to his military duties, which in this climate does not answer at all. I have been allowed to see her the last week. The physician who attends her cannot understand her malady at all, but calls it nervous irritability. We all say if he flogged her round the room three times in the morning and ditto in the evening she would soon be well. She is the victim of indulgence and a nasty disposition.

Friday July 1st   I wish you could have seen a specimen of the Calcutta gentry in the shape of a lady who called upon us this morning with her husband. He is as deaf as a post and only hears through the medium of a long tube which he throws at you. This woman was once a cook. Upon this occasion she was drest Oh! so fine, with little plaistered oval curls stuck tight upon her forehead, besides lovely ones which hung down on the side. Her bonnet was put well back on her head to facilitate the display of two gold combs. She was rouged to the eyes, and her mouth was saying 'stewed prunes'. Her person was enveloped in white and blue, and in her hand she carried a feather fan. She started by saying, 'Mr Greenlaw is quite deaf, but it does not signify, I always engross the whole of the conversation myself'; and indeed she never spoke a truer word, for not a syllable could one get in edgewise. But to give you an idea of her would be impossible, and to keep one's countenance at her equally so. Before she had well left the room I burst into a roar of laughter. The husband is a nice, amiable-looking old man, but neither Christine nor I could summon up resolution to ask for the end of his tube, so there he sat, poor beast, without uttering, to our everlasting disgrace.

We stopped some itinerant tumblers today to amuse ourselves with. They only did one wonderful feat, which was this. A very high bamboo was reared up, I suppose about 20 feet high. Upon the tip top of this was an iron spike about a foot in length. The man first of all got up to the top just like a monkey, and when he reached the spike, this he applied to his stomach (of course he had a plate of some sort inside his girdle), spread out his upper and lower extremities and so *spun* round and round just like a teetotum. All of us with the exception of John thought it very extraordinary, but his love of an argument is such that when a person states an opinion he instantly takes the other side, and we frequently catch him contradicting his position of a previous day for the sake of opposition. He is a very odd being, but the best-tempered fellow I ever saw.

Wednesday 6th   Christine a little wrong, but no wonder, for the system she pursues with the baby is quite enough to kill anyone else. She has up to this moment nursed it totally and entirely herself, which in this country is an unheard-of thing. Then the child from its birth has slept in the bed with her, which as long as it had no intellect did not signify, but now that it has does very much. The little monster sleeps like a top until she steps into bed, but as soon as she comes it begins to fidget and will not rest unless she has it in her arms and is nursing it every hour the whole night through. The consequence of this is that from being in the habit of sleeping all the night long, three hours of broken sleep is the average of what she now gets, which in this climate is ruin to one. I am afraid I should make a shocking mama, for I confess I cannot understand how having a fat maggot by one's side can compensate for the loss of one's comfortable rest.

Sunday 10th Went to church, so that you see in spite of its being the rainy season, one can get out. Indeed, I am most agreeably surprised about the rains, for I expected it was to pour night and day without ceasing for two or three months, but there are great cessations between the storms and we have only been as yet prevented about twice from taking our evening drive. I am afraid that now, at the moment I am writing, this calamity will befall us for the third time. I went after church to see unfortunate Mrs Beresford. I do not like it, for she makes me cry. I sincerely wish she was off. She is quite distracted at leaving Marc, yet feels she will die if she remains. She will sail in about a month.

Tuesday 12th This morning Christine and I were occupied from ten till one at the Town Hall in arranging things on a table for a fancy sale which was to take place the following day for the benefit of some schools here. We were requested to take a table, which as a duty we consented to do. It was very fatiguing work, and we came home with aching feet and streaming faces.

Wednesday 13th   The sale began at ten. I dreaded it very much, for I thought I should make some confusion in the accounts, never having undertaken an affair of the sort before. However, it did very well. We made excellent shop girls and puffed off our goods in such fine style that our table produced more than any of the others. We got about 400 rupees, i.e., £40, and when one considers the rubbish we had to sell I think it was doing pretty well. Several natives attended. One very polite fellow, so beautifully drest, announced he wished particularly to make some purchases at our table, which he did accordingly. There were others also, but they were monsters and tried to bate down our articles.

Ships have arrived and brought us letters, but none from you this time. I do not repine, for you behave nobly to me. Now with love to all believe me ever yours

Very affectionately,

I. Fane

VI

July 15th Friday   I was to have gone today to
Barrackpore with my father, but the storms of rain were
so violent I was afraid to venture – the more so, as he
was going in his break, which is a very unprotected
machine in rain. We were going for the purpose of
crossing the river the following morning, to see an
indigo factory belonging to a bankrupt estate of Mr
Holroyd's. My father, having a portion of his farming
or agricultural propensities left, was anxious to see the
process of indigo manufacture from beginning to end.
He started at a little after five in the evening with Mr
Holroyd and John, after a violent pour down of rain. I
am glad *I* did not, for although it did not rain very much
between the hours of five and seven, yet it never ceased,
more or less, and this is not pleasant weather to go out
visiting in.

Henry, Christine, Captain Campbell and I were left at
home. As we were quietly seated a little before nine
o'clock, digesting whether or no we would play a
rubber of whist or a pool of écarté, a black man came
running into the room in great perturbation to tell us
Major Macan was very ill. We all rushed downstairs
immediately. The gentlemen went into his room and
found he had broken a blood vessel and was vomiting
up much blood. We instantly sent off for doctors and in
about five minutes two were in the house. In about an
hour, by means of ice, the haemorrhage was stopped,

but in his dreadful state it became a question whether he would live through the night. We therefore judged it right to send an express to my father to state particulars, and he, upon the strength of what we said, returned home the following morning, on account, in case he died, of the funeral; for in this country you must be buried within twenty-four hours after your decease. However, he is alive today and, all things considered, wonderfully well, and still has hopes of his ultimate recovery. He has lately been under the care of a native doctor, and has made a wonderful rally – from the effect upon his mind more than the remedies he has used. He is such a sight to behold, and the living skeleton was a joke to him.

Saturday 16th July   Major Macan alive. His brother is to be sent for, who has a situation up the country, not very far off. He is a very religious man. Major Macan is not fond of him; but he is not fond of anyone. I am delighted he is coming. For me there is something so dreadful in the unfortunate man's situation, to be dying without a creature to offer him consolation or smooth his pillows if for a moment even he felt he should like care or attention. The tiresome rain came on this evening just as we were going out to drive and we were prevented from budging.

Sunday 17th   We went to church this morning – only John and I. There was to be a sermon and collection afterwards for the distressed clergy in Ireland. A cause was never worse pleaded, but I do not know what the result was. This evening we passed in spelling words with my beautiful letters, which Mr Melville gave me; and although it sounds a childish

93

amusement, the hour from dinner to bedtime passed quickly. Major Macan alive and tolerable.

Monday 18th   I went to spend the morning with the Misses Eden. I was rather bored, for I did not feel in a humour for the thing. I came home in our palanquin. It was the first time I had been so far in one, and I liked it very much. I could fancy it a charming conveyance for night travelling were it not for the constant stoppages which take place. The poor bearers change shoulders every five minutes, and if one happened to be asleep and this woke one each time it would prove unpleasant. This evening at Mrs Campbell Robertson's. She is Mrs Elliott's daughter. They are famous for their stinginess and the shocking dinners they give. What there is on the table is very bad of its sort, and not sufficient for the mouths or stomachs that are to be filled. On our return home we found that poor Major Macan had broken another blood vessel and had bled more than before. His situation is truly melancholy. He has never been to bed since Thursday night, but is propped up in a chair with a table attached to it before him, on which he rests his arms and head. He has at length quite given himself up and is awaiting most patiently his end. I think, I hope, the extraordinary patience with which he has borne his long and protracted illness must cover a multitude of his sins. I never saw so patient a sufferer.

Wednesday 20th   I was to drive with Miss F. Eden. Just after we started the rain came on. We took refuge in Government House, and after a little exercise of patience we were enabled to start again and got a mouthful of air, with some rain also. We had some people to dinner. Mrs T. Prinsep and her stomach was the only lady. We are excellent friends now and her manners are so improved, although she made both myself and Christine very angry, for she chose to discuss the young ladies of this city. If you could but have heard the things she said of every man John of them! They were so spiteful – so much so that although we don't care a sou for one of them we took the line of calling them all angels. She errs dreadfully in this respect, but she is so obliging. We had some men besides, who played a rubber of whist with my father.

Friday 22nd   My father has got a touch of the gout and a bad sneezing cold in his head. The former we attribute to Mr Robertson's sour claret of Monday, the latter to the damp of the atmosphere. But he is not much amiss and will be well in a few days. Fancy what satisfaction I must have felt this morning upon opening a tin box in which I had most carefully packed up, in flannel and waxed cloth, all my silk dresses which I had worn during the cold weather, only to find them every one totally ruined. It is most particularly vexatious for I thought I had a sufficient stock for my up-country expedition, and now I must buy more, and I am totally ruined, without a rupee in the world, I have indulged so much in little things in the ornamental way. But I do not care about this, for I see no good in being the Commander-in-Chief's daughter if I may not indulge now that he is wallowing in wealth. He will not complain, I am sure, for he is very liberal. I went at five o'clock this evening with Marc and his little child to see some antic people at Government House. It was a very stupid exhibition. I went out driving afterwards with Miss F. Eden, and whilst she was putting on her bonnet Lord Auckland politely took me into a room and staid with me. I was so very much amused at him inwardly. I am certain in his own mind he thought I should make *him* an offer, he looked so sheepish and foolish, and so relieved when Miss F. Eden made her appearance. How much he mistook his man if it did cross his imagination!

Sunday 24th   John and I went to church. John slept all the time, but he had been picnicking for three days previous, with some of his pet young ladies, and had not gone to bed until two o'clock on Saturday night. My father is better but not quite well. Poor Major Macan died this evening at about eight o'clock, without a struggle. He broke another blood vessel, which he had not strength to get rid of and was suffocated in three minutes. His brother was with him, which was a great comfort. This event, although we all disliked him prodigiously, threw a great damp over us as you may suppose. Both Christine and I as bed time advanced felt very nervous, for which I think we were great fools, and I actually made my maid sleep in the room with me. This is a favourable moment to say I like my new maid very much. She speaks Hindostanee beautifully and understands the ways of these people perfectly.

Monday 25th   At half-past five this evening poor Major Macan's funeral took place. It was immensely attended by military, and it sounded so dreadfully melancholy and impressive. As the hearse moved off the band struck up some dismal and solemn air.

Tuesday 26th   This morning Christine and I and Captain Campbell went to pay some morning visits. The first was very unpropitious. After being denied we were then let in, and after having been kept waiting half an hour the lady, who is a nice lady, made her appearance *en robe de chambre*, evidently not having been made aware of the presence of an A.D.C. or gentleman;

and as she is about to have a baby (as every lady here is) she was a very disgraceful sight. She was very unwell, so we speedily took our departure.

Thursday 28th   I paid Mrs Beresford a visit and found her as usual; a shade better, but very bad and looking shockingly and most anxious for a ship to arrive to take her away. At five o'clock I started for Barrackpore and had such a nice cool drive. There is no one here but the family, and as I am now more intimate I am enjoying myself.

Saturday 30th   We had some people to dinner today and a juggler in the evening, who boasted much of his exploits. But he proved a complete humbug, for he did nothing but eat glass (nearly the whole of three glass bottles) and a certain portion of fire, and make a rupee walk about the room; but there was great imposition in all, and we all agreed he ought to have been horse-whipped.

Sunday 31st   No church at Barrackpore; the clergyman sick, and clergymen are scarce articles in this country. Poor Miss Eden is very low about Lord Melbourne and Mrs Norton. The former is a very great friend of hers so she is much distressed at his immorality.

Monday August 1st   I left Barrackpore this morning at eight o'clock and did not reach Calcutta until ten, which was much too late in the day to be on the road. I am sorry to say I found my father very ill, with much fever, entirely in consequence of his own imprudence.

Contrary to all advice he would hold his levée on Saturday, being far from well in the morning. I found him on Monday with lots of leeches on his head, behind his ears, to subdue the great pain he had there. I am happy to say they have had the desired effect, for all fever has now left him and he has only strength to pick up. As soon as he is strong enough to be moved he will go somewhere for a change of air; and in about another month now we shall move from this bad climate to the best in the world. You need not be the least alarmed about this attack; my father is quite out of danger, I assure you, and, please God, will be well in a few days more.

Friday 5th   Today we were to have a large dinner party; early it was to be, because my father patronized a theatrical entertainment for the good of Mrs Leach, the milliner and actress, given at the Town Hall. As my father was out of all danger and much better, he would not have it put off, so we sat down sixteen at a quarter before six and notwithstanding the absence of the master it went off very well. There was plenty of talking and plenty of food, and at a little after seven we all sallied forth to the scene of action. Upon our arrival we found everything so badly managed that we had difficulty in getting seats at all, and as to reserving any for the Commander-in-Chief, the liberty-and-equality people here would not hear of it, and we were all in a predicament. I got a seat at last next to the Governor-General, but anything to equal the heat we had to endure it is impossible to conceive; notwithstanding which I was very much amused. We had the farce of *The Liar* [unidentified] and after it *High, Low, Jack and the Game* [unidentified], both well got up, the performers being chiefly amateurs. It lasted until nearly twelve o'clock, and I thought I must have slept in my clothes. I was in such a heat that they stuck to me like wax. The weather now is dreadfully oppressive. It always is during the months of August and September, but it is more so than usual this year on account of the irregularity and deficiency of the rains. It is rather odd that whilst in the act of writing this sentence such a shower has commenced, and although it is much cooler in consequence, the thermometer is standing at 84. I forgot to look at it before.

I do believe I forgot to note down on the proper day, *viz* Wednesday the 3rd, that Mrs Thoby Prinsep produced a fine boy. We have had such fun since the event took place in our correspondence of enquiry. She has an unmarried sister nursing her, who has been living with her of late.★ Because, I believe, she is so disgusted with her father, Jemmy Blaze, she is very unhappy at home. This creature, Miss Julia by name, sets up for a *bas-bleu* and the notes she writes in answer to our commonplace enquiries are worth reading. She says in one, after enquiring about my father, "many in this house will make offerings at the shrine of Aesculapius upon his recovery"!! She makes me so sick, and she is so ugly and so conceited withal.

Saturday 6th   My father sat up today from four till eight and ate mutton for his dinner. I went to see Mrs Beresford and found her in the same state. It is finally arranged that she sails in the *Perfect* on the 20th; which ship, by the bye, will probably convey this to you.

August 10th   News is so scarce now, so are anecdotes. What have I got to tell you since the 6th, for I am in arrears? Why, that my father has progressed daily.

★ The future Mrs Cameron. See pp 33 and 61.

He has taken two evening drives, and after his excursion to the Sandheads he will be as well as ever. The last two days have been great days of bustle, for quantities of horses, carriages, clothes etc., have been sent off in boats up to Allahabad to be ready for our arrival there. We had a visit today from Mr Macan, poor Major Macan's brother. He is such a dolorous looking man, but he was in better spirits than I expected to have seen him, as this was our first interview since the death of the other. There came also a little cadet from England of the name of Harris, with a letter in his pocket from Mrs Ellice. If she is in reach, tell her I wish she would not send her hobbydy boys here to stay hours with us! He seemed a gentleman–like boy, but I daresay she knows nothing of either him or his parents further than that the papa probably has a vote in the Directory business!

Thursday 11th   My father went away this morning at six o'clock to embark on board the steamer. John and Dr Wood went with him. Henry and his wife and I are left behind. I did not go because he intends shooting out for three hours and three hours back again into the Bay of Bengal, and this is a rough time of year for this purpose. As I am so bad a sailor, I should have been neither useful nor ornamental. We heard today of Henry [Edward] Fane being in the river, but snugly stuck at a place called *Mud Point*. I mention this because he cannot well come to any harm; otherwise I should not. A young man, a nephew of Colonel Beresford's, came in the same ship with him from Madras and dined with us today; but Henry did not choose to leave the ship until it came to its moorings, off Calcutta, so he has not yet made his appearance. I have done all I can to facilitate his arrival at our house, and I hope he will join our dinner party today.

Friday 12th   We had a little dinner party of our own this evening. Colonel and Mrs Torrens dined with us. He is Adjutant-General of the King's troops – a fat, croaking old stupe. His wife is reckoned a *sweet* woman, but she is so like a governess that one cannot get on with her. They are just starting for up the country, being a part of the staff; and as their house was all to pieces, we thought they would get no dinner if we did not ask them.

Saturday 13th   Henry made his appearance to breakfast this morning. He is quite well, and tumbles into all Major Macan's clothes, and as all he wants of them fit him very well he is much pleased, and not *frightened*, as *I* should be at wearing a dead man's clothes, for fear of his ghost haunting me. Mrs Beresford's only brother, the young man who was staying with her for some weeks on her first arrival here, died a few days ago. It is a sad calamity, and would be at any time, but it is a particularly heavy one just now to poor Marc, who was very, very fond of the poor young man. In consequence of her state Mrs Beresford must not be told of it, so poor Marc has all the anguish for his early death to feel and conceal.

Tuesday 16th   Today I received your packet of March 29th. I am so disappointed at all the questions you ask me about our establishment, the dress of the servants, etc., etc. I thought I had told you all this at first. However, I will discuss the matter now, and if a journal should turn up with any description, you must excuse my twice-told tale. The number of servants my father keeps, who wait upon him and me, is sixty-eight, and this is reckoned a *small* number for the Commander-in-Chief. Other C. in C.s have had more. But besides these

101

there are in the house about sixteen of Henry's, male and female. By the bye, four of these belong to the stable. John has eight or nine, Captain Campbell ditto, Henry ditto, Dr. Wood ditto, and Christine's maid, and mine, have each their man to wait upon them! I will dress up a figure to send you of the style of dress worn by the servants in this country, which is so very picturesque and pretty. At dinner I have three khitmagurs or waiting servants behind my chair. My father has *six* to his portion, everyone else one or two. Then there is the khansamar or butler, the plate butler, the wine cooler and his mate, the jelly maker, and many whose avocations I know nothing about; but I should think at our meals we are when *quite alone* surrounded by nearer thirty much, than twenty. All these are Mussalman [Muslims]; no other caste will touch our food. These *will* put port on the table, but I am told if you venture on any part of the pig you had better not reflect upon it, for they look upon the pig as an unclean beast and if compelled to put on the table any part of the animal would not scruple to *spit* on it first!

No room in India has such a thing as a bell. Figures squat outside your door called hurakarus [*harakara* – messenger] and when you want anything you call out *quy hi!* [*koi hai* – 'is anyone there?'] and one of these comes. They are Hindoos always, and will bring you a candle, go of messages, fetch and carry notes; but if you want some water to put a bouquet in, a plate taken away, or a bit of paste, they must go and fetch a khitmagur to do it, as it would be against their caste. Naked figures called bearers make your bed and dust the room; but they are very particular about their caste, so much so that if a *certain* little *stand*, into which you put a certain machine, happens to stand so near the bed that they cannot get to it without coming into contact with this, they go away and call a lady who acts in the capacity of housemaid, and who is looked upon as the dregs of the earth because she does all your dirty work for you. I think now I have told you all you have asked; of course there remains much more to be told, but then if I were to tell all I *could*, I had better publish a book. The nights have become so hot I have taken to a punkah in bed, and the luxury of it is not to be told. It is the only cool time one enjoys throughout the twenty-four hours. I can bear a sheet over me, and wake in the morning as cool as a cucumber and quite fresh, instead of feeling tired and languid as I did before.

Tuesday 16th   Today we dined at five o'clock because there were to have been fine doings at Government House. A *corps dramatique* from France have just arrived here, and were to exhibit their talents for the first time at G. House. The prima donna, unfortunately, was taken ill, and the play was postponed in consequence; and as the evening was to end in a common 'at home' such as they have every fortnight (not one of which I have ever been to), we all agreed that the evening was so hot we would stay at home and play our casino as usual. We are, i.e., Christine and I, and Captain Campbell and Dr Wood, become very attached to this game, and play at it for all sorts of odd things, such as ribbons, shaving brushes, gloves, Delhi scarves, China handkerchiefs, riding whips, etc., etc. We get so excited we are almost rude to one another. Good accounts from the Ganges steamer of my father. He had had no fever for two days.

Wednesday 17th   Very good accounts today from my father. He would have staid at sea for a few days more, but unfortunately they have expended their coals and must return tomorrow. This evening I intended to take a ride with the two Henrys, Mr Holroyd having lent me such a lovely Arab, which he assured me was perfectly quiet. Well, I mounted it in gallant style and set off, but it went in a manner that put me into a sort of heat that you perishing creatures in England cannot fancy. So having gone the length of the street about, off I jumped and stepped into the carriage, which fortunately happened to be just before me. We ended the evening with casino and went to bed a little after ten. I have left off eating dinner at eight o'clock. I have tea and toast instead and dine at two, and you cannot think how much more comfortable I have felt since.*

Thursday 18th   We determined this morning to go and pay a duty call at Government House, Thursday being the Misses Eden's receiving day. We found many assembled, and as the result was neither pleasure nor profit we shortly took our leave. We took Henry with us (I mean Mrs E. Fane's Henry, whom we mean to call Le Gros, to distinguish him from the *three* others in the house already) to introduce him. We buttoned him up in his scarlet coat etc., etc. and I assure you Christine and I expected to swim about the carriage, the *pers* streamed off him in such a manner! From thence we went to see some fine native jewellery which is for sale and which I would not have given anything I already possess in exchange for. There was one immense diamond, valued at I know not what, that looked to me for all the world

---

* Many observers attributed the 'fevers' and 'liver' complaints from which the British constantly suffered to their refusal to adapt their diet to the climate. 'Everybody about me', wrote Victor Jacquemont, 'continues to eat his three meals, religiously abstaining from mixing any water with the heaviest wines of Spain and Portugal. Then, when evening brings a little coolness, they get on horseback and young and old gallop aimlessly for an hour like automatons; they return home drenched with perspiration and, as a preparation for sleeping lightly and easily at night, sit down to table, where they remain for two hours, only leaving it to go to bed.' (*Letters from India,* p.15)

like the drop of a lustre. We then paid a visit, or did our best to do so, and returned home to tear off our clothes and endeavour to get cool for luncheon. My father returned home at six o'clock, having derived the greatest benefit from the change. He still keeps invalid hours, such as dining at two, drinking tea instead of a second dinner and going to bed very early.

Friday 19th   My father got up this morning as fresh as a lark and took an early drive, before seven o'clock I mean. We are only so fearful of his returning to his *hard* work too soon, but we all try our utmost to prevent it. Miss Frances Eden paid us a visit and made herself so agreeable. Edward Hodges arrived, having broken up partnership with Mr Harris. He is looking ill; but no doubt this circumstance has worried him and caused it, for he is such an excellent creature that I have not the least doubt he cannot settle *himself* quite whether he has acted right in quitting Mr Harris's service. We can for him very easily. People exist in great measure to get on in life, and why is he to sacrifice his chances to oblige a person who has not very particularly considered him? And now with best love to everyone I love, believe me yours very affectionately as well as gratefully for all your delightful budgets,

Isabella Fane.

VII

Calcutta, August 28th, 1836   In what a melancholy
manner must this journal begin. Exactly the very day
and month commemorative of the death of poor Major
Macan, poor Mrs Beresford breathed her last, at half-
past eleven o'clock on Saturday night. She most
undoubtedly, poor creature, has fallen a victim to the
climate of Bengal. But the circumstance does not alarm
any one of us, and pray do not let it alarm you, or
anyone else who feels affection for us, for the truth is
that in her case there has been as large a mixture of folly
and weakness as the effects of climate. For a great many
weeks it had been quite evident that if she remained here
she must die, and it had also been quite arranged that she
was to return to England. After all this was arranged
many ships took their departure which on account of
their tonnage were not approved of, as not affording
sufficiently good accommodation, until, alas, it was put
off too long, and when the *Perfect*, which was at length
the ship fixed upon, was ready for sailing, she poor
thing was in such a state she could not be moved.
Although the Captain was most kind, and even waited
in hopes that she might rally, it was all ineffectual, and
she died of exhaustion from dysentery the night before
the ship sailed. She had not one organic affection, her
liver was not in the least affected. Latterly she had a very
bad cough, but this had nothing to do with her lungs; it
was an affection of the windpipe. Conceive, for the last

106

two months she has never been able to bear a breath of
air to blow upon her, either from the heavens or by the
means of a punkah; and during all this dreadfully hot
weather one may truly say she has perspired away her
existence. I have been to sit with her when I have been
ready to die from the heat, with only my dressing gown
and chemise on, and she also has been sopping from the
same cause; but still she fancied a punkah made her
worse.

I am sure you who have a feeling heart will pity the
poor bereft husband. She died at half-past eleven, and
at six in the morning the poor father put his little child
on board the *Perfect* to send to England, having put his
own feelings quite out of the question, judging it best
for the little creature so to do. I could break my heart
when I think of the poor little child, which has been
much spoilt by both its parents, torn from them both
and sent upon a long, long journey with two people
whom it never saw before. I saw her the Wednesday
before she died, and kissed her, as she was to have been
put on board the following day. Then I did not at all
despair of her, although she was very, very bad. Poor
Marc is at present much better than one could expect,
but when all is quite over and her poor body
committed to the earth will be the dreadful calm and
time when he will feel his loneliness. God help him,
poor fellow.

Sunday 29th   This evening, at about five o'clock,
poor Mrs Beresford was committed to her last home.
Her funeral was perfectly private, by Marc's desire, no
one attending but himself, my brother and John Michel.
I have nothing to relate between Sunday and this time,
unless indeed for the information of Mrs Edward Fane I
mention that Edward Hodges has been in Calcutta for
the last week to prepare for his departure to his new

employment. Mirzeffapore [Muzaffarpur] is the place he is bound to, and if I recollect right this is the place where the W. Fanes lived at the time that drawing was done which is in Mrs Fane's album. He seems very much delighted at the field before him, and I hope, poor fellow, he will get on. He is an excellent good creature and deserving of success. Mr Harris has not *quarrelled* with him, but is not pleased at his having withdrawn himself from his concern. He started this morning (Thursday 1st September) by steam for his destination. My father sent away poor Marc also by the same flat, to Allahabad, there to await our arrival.

I have not written in my journal for an immense time, because I have had so much to do, which you will understand as I proceed. I will collect my scattered thoughts and see whether anything has occurred in the mean time worth relating. We dined one day at Government House, a mere union of the two families; at least, there was one stranger, a Mr Blunt, ex-Governor of Agra, and I could not find out whether it was Lady Seton's brother, who, it is said, has behaved so ill to her in money matters. If he is the same, it is very odd, for he has the reputation of being most particularly liberal and has behaved, or rather is behaving, towards some members of his wife's family in an out-of-the-way liberal manner, laying aside a large sum annually for the purpose of educating some nephews and nieces who have been by some accident left in a forlorn state. But our dinner party was very dull. After dinner we had a casino party and a backgammon party. I played with Mr Holroyd and Miss Frances Eden in the latter and won a curious little figure in ivory from China, which I have carefully put away.

For the last ten days our time has been completely occupied in packing. If we had not done it by degrees I do not know where we should have been. We each in our respective ways had so much. At last came the day of our departure, *viz* yesterday, Tuesday the 13th of September. At a little before ten o'clock we had completely finished with the Bishop's Palace, so we all got into our various vehicles and proceeded to Mrs Thoby Prinsep's, where we all (with the exception of John, on account of what I before told you of him and her) went to breakfast. It was odd that at her house we breakfasted on our arrival in Calcutta, and at hers breakfasted on our departure from it, death having removed in the interval two of our party. We remained at her house doing nothing until past one o'clock. In the meantime the Governor-General's carriages had arrived to convey us to the riverside. Into these we stepped and drove through the fort, which is said by connoisseurs to be the prettiest possible. The drive through this was a very pretty sight. All the troops were out, both native and European, and formed a line on each side of us the whole length of the fort, with their bands playing and colours flying. On the banks of the river the Governor-General's barge was waiting, which was to convey us on board our Noah's Ark or flat, and we finally started at about two o'clock. We have arranged all our rooms quite as comfortably as circumstances will permit. Mine is twelve feet long and nine wide, and is one of the best. The heat is terrific at present, but it is to be cooler, they say, soon. We only got as far as Barrackpore the first night, and then anchored.

Wednesday 14th   We let go our anchor at break of day and got on very well until about three o'clock, when we stuck in a bank. The stream is so strong at this season that we are obliged to keep under the bank (or in slack water). This accounts for the accident. We only remained a few minutes in this predicament, and then got off easily. We were at dinner at the time. We anchored at sunset at no place, and my rest was much disturbed by a flight of musquitoes which were allowed to get into my bed. The insects of all sorts and kinds are very troublesome. We breakfast at nine, dine at half-past two, drink tea at about six, and go to bed at about ten, first playing some rubbers at casino. We are now forming a fund in order to buy something pretty at the first place we stop at, and we shall then play a game of fright for it.

Thursday 15th This morning upon endeavouring to start at daylight we found ourselves in such a strong current, which was against us, that we could not stir. We were five hours doing nothing but swinging round. At length we were enabled to cross the stream into slack water, and we then got on. At dinner time we passed a large native town called Culna, in which the Rajah of Birdwan resides. He has a very fine house in which he stows away his person. We anchored at sunset off a piece of ground chosen expressly by my father for the accommodation of our Hindoo servants, that they might be put on shore to cook and eat their victuals. Their religion forbids their doing anything of the kind on their sacred river, and when they cannot go on shore they eat nothing but dry rice. On shore they make a little fireplace of clay in a minute, make some fire, and cook a nice curry. All the gentlemen went also for a short time to stretch their limbs and look about them; but they were not rewarded for their trouble. They saw nothing but a few quail and one snake. The banks are frightful all the way yet – so perfectly flat, and no variety of landscape. The heat is tremendous. My room at about four o'clock p.m. was 94. We ended the evening with casino; went to bed piping hot and so remained all night. My father is quite well and it is beautiful to see how idle he is by comparison.

Friday 16th   We went on very prosperously throughout this day. The banks of the river frightful on each side. In consequence of the manner in which the whole country is inundated (it being now the last month of the rainy season) we passed today up several nullahs, or narrow passages, formed by the floods, which saved us several miles of our voyage. Our anchorage tonight was not far from a native village, but it was amongst trees, so we could not see it. There were also a number of native boats which chose this spot for their anchorage, and they were very disagreeable neighbours. It is such a talkative nation, and these good people never ceased all night either talking or uttering unearthly noises. I did not like their near neighbourhood, for I expected to wake and find a black figure getting in at my window - which was, I believe, an unnecessary alarm, for we have a sentry pacing the deck night and day, with orders to allow nothing to approach our Noah's ark. But still, if you could only see how near our windows are to the water's edge, you would not be surprised at my alarm. Some of the gentlemen went on shore, John amongst the number. He went to the village; but both men and women were alarmed. The latter ran away as fast as they could go, upon which I ventured to hint to him that his character had preceded him! At Calcutta it was so gone he was the terror of the modest and well-behaved and the ruin of the tender-hearted!

Saturday 17th   The banks of the river this morning for several hours were much prettier than anything we have before passed, but only on account of trees; no elevation of ground. Nothing occurred worth putting on paper during this day. We anchored at sunset off a piece of ground which enabled the Hindoos to cook and the gentlemen to go on shore. John took his gun and shot three birds of the duck kind, but they were only fit food for a Mussulman, not for a Christian. His beaters were his moonshie, or man who is teaching him Hindostanee and Arabic, his barber, and one of the khitmagurs or attending servants. The baby and its attendants also went on shore to exercise. The poor little thing has been shockingly naughty ever since it came on board, by night and by day. During the former it suffers so much from heat it cannot be too good; and during the day with this, and seeing all of us every half minute, it does nothing but whine and cry to get to us; besides, it is cutting its teeth. We are come to anchor at a very pretty spot, and I have just been to Henry (*Le Gros* as we call him) to insist upon his taking a sketch of it. He is very able with his pencil, and I mean to brush him up. A Hindoo has just finished his prayers and ablutions opposite my window, and an odd process it is, but not at all imposing. It only consists of taking a little water in the hands, putting them up and making marks on the face, something in the way the clergyman does when he christens a child. We land this evening after sunset at Bherampore [Barhampur], which is the place where Mr Melville resides. We are all to drink tea with him, and sleep with him. Tomorrow morning my father reviews some troops; we sleep with Mr Melville again that night and re-embark the following morning at daybreak. All this takes in Sunday the 18th, Monday 19th and Tuesday 20th. I am obliged to anticipate these few days because my father sends off letters from Bherampore this evening. So I shall conclude this by informing you we are all perfectly well, that I send my love to all friends, and will you tell Mrs Fane, with my

most affectionate love, that I shall prepare a letter to
send to her from the next place we stop at. Believe me,
my dear Mrs Chaplin,

Yours very affectionately,

I. Fane.

On the river in a great perspiration this good Sunday,
September 18th, 1836

PART TWO: ON TOUR

PART TWO: ON TOUR

VIII

September 18th 1836   My dear Mrs Chaplin, when I concluded my last journal I was obliged to do so in a hurry because we were to land on that day and my father was going to make up his packet to send to England; so I take up the pith of my tale from that very day. Well, between four and five o'clock in the afternoon we reached Bherampore. On the shore were crowds of natives to see us land; but Mr Melville and the officers of the regiment quartered in the place were the only Europeans. A salute was fired. We anchored only a few yards from the shore and Mr Melville's house was only a few yards further, so Christine and I got into tonjohns [*tamjham* – a kind of sedan chair on a single pole, carried by four bearers]. The gentlemen walked with chattahs [*chhattar* – umbrella] held over their heads. We found Mr Melville looking in excellent health. He is grown so fat, with two stomachs and two chins. He lives in the cantonments, which, in consequence of there being no European regiments now allowed to stay at Bherampore, are unoccupied. About ten years (or even less I believe) ago this was reckoned a very unhealthy station; but a change has taken place, and if we are to judge by Mr Melville's appearance one would pronounce it the Montpellier of India. His quarters are not at all nice; so very hot and stuffy, without the possibility of a breath of air getting into the house even when the gods are pleased to order a small portion to

117

blow, which they certainly did not whilst we were there. We suffered at night from the heat quite as much as we had done on board the flat. As soon as the sun permitted that evening, Mr Melville supplied us with carriages and horses and we took a very nice and pretty drive. We had no company that evening, dined quietly and went to our roasting beds in good time.

Monday 19th   This morning at daybreak my father was to have inspected the handful of troops (native) quartered here; but there had been a tremendous thunder storm with torrents of rain during the night, which had so wet the ground it was postponed until the afternoon. All the civil and military characters in the place came to call upon my father in the course of the morning, and as they had to pass through the room in which we ladies sat, we also had the benefit of their society. This place is celebrated for its workers in thorn, and beautiful things we saw there, such as chess men, boxes, palanquins, puzzles, paper-cutters and many others. We purchased a very pretty carved work box for our pool of casino, and a very pretty little thing to stand on one's table, *viz* one of the carts of the country drawn by bullocks. At a little after five the inspection took place, and I believe the appearance of the men and their manoeuvring met with the approbation of His Excellency. Here I will take the opportunity of saying you cannot think how popular my father is as Commander-in-Chief. It is said of him he has the interest of the army so thoroughly at heart and that ere long it will begin to recover the great injuries done it by that plague spot of India, Lord William Bentinck. It is not prejudice makes me say this. John tells me these pleasant remarks as they are made to him, and of course they must be the sincere feelings of individuals, for they could not have a motive in making them to John. At a little before six we all started, intending to see the whole process of manufacturing the silk for which this place is also famed, known here by the appellation of cossimbazar silks. Quantities of those yellow and red figured pocket handkerchiefs which are so prized in England are manufactured here, besides gown pieces, but these latter have not much to recommend them. We were disappointed this evening of seeing this, for the carriage conveying my father and Mr Melville met with an accident, which detained them *en route*, and it became too dark. We therefore returned home very late for dinner. I had to dress in a tremendous hurry, which is perfect wretchedness in this climate, and rush into a room where twenty-six people were assembled. I sat next to Mr Melville and some major, who was a pleasant man, and the dinner as far as I was concerned went off pleasantly. They drank toasts after the ladies retired and made a great noise. Went to bed in very good time and had a roasting night.

Tuesday 20th   We got up at five o'clock this morning for we had much to do. First we went to see the silk manufacture which we had been disappointed about the night before. It was very amusing and put one in mind of the days of our youth when we kept silk worms and a little machine for winding the silk etc., etc., for we saw all this. After this we went on the Moorshedabad [Murshidabad], which is eight miles from Bherampore, for the purpose of seeing a most magnificent palace which is being built there in the English style for the Nawab of Bengal. It has been entirely planned by a Colonel Macleod, a nice gentleman-like old soldier, who is very proud of it, as well he may be. It is in the Doric style of architecture, and puts one much in mind of Sandhurst and Whitehall. Christine and I wanted very much to see the Begum. Mr Melville and Colonel

Macleod said we might, and were going to manage it for us, but my father did not approve the plan and would not let us. We breakfasted at Colonel Macleod's and had an excellent meal. About two hours afterwards the steamer reached Moorshedabad and we re-embarked. It is much further from Bherampore by water than by land, you will understand.

Wednesday 21st   This morning on waking we caught sight of the Rajmahal hills at a great distance. We had been anticipating these with interest, as they were the first elevations we had seen since we entered Bengal. The more we advanced, the more distinct they became, and they form a beautiful background to the otherwise ugly landscape. Between twelve and one o'clock we entered the famed Ganges and I went on deck at the propitious moment. The river is about three miles wide at this point, where it becomes the actual Ganges. The first branch we came up, from Calcutta to Nuddya, is called the Hooghly [Hughli]; we then entered the Bhagruttee [Bhagirati], and finally the Ganges. We met with neither adventure nor misadventure until eleven and twelve at night, when a tremendous storm of wind and rain came on, and as the damage we had met with a few days previous had not up to this time been repaired, it proved most inconvenient.* My sleeping apartment was inundated and I was obliged to leave it and my bed and make my escape to our sitting room and lie down on my couch, there a victim to musquitoes until the storm was over. We were driven by the current close upon a mud bank, upon which I could have stepped

---

* In her diary entry for Tuesday 20th she writes: 'In the course of this day we met with a bad accident. In consequence of the strong current, we ran foul of a native boat and tore off with a frightful crash almost every Venetian blind on one side of our flat.'

Isabella Fane

View of Calcutta from the Esplanade

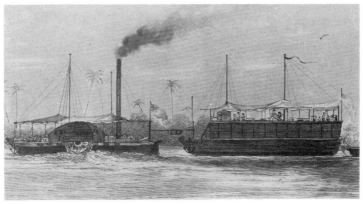

Steamboat on the Ganges

Country shipping on the Ganges

The palace at Agra

The principal street of Agra

Simla in the 1830s

Simla in the 1830s

A view of Delhi

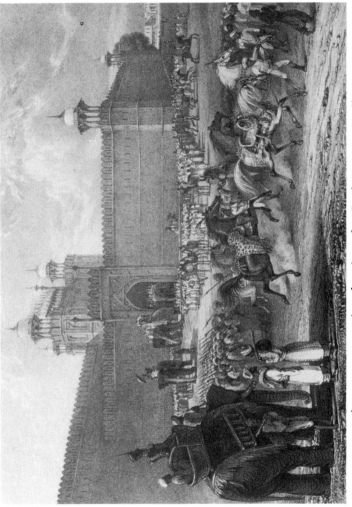

A state procession leaving the Red Fort in Delhi

A *janpan* ('jonpaun') and the Commander-in-Chief's
tents. Two sketches by Isabella Fane

with the greatest facility, and I could not but think how foolish we should look if an alligator or some wild beast chose to pay us a visit. However, after a bit the storm ceased, I went back to my bed and we resumed our voyage at daybreak without any damage having been done.

Thursday 22nd   We had throughout the day an increasing view of the Rajmahal hills, as we kept approaching them. They put me in mind of the hills about Poole and Salisbury. They are famous for tigers and afford good sport in this way, but our own gentlemen are not to be allowed to try their skill. Rather before sunset we anchored a little short of the town of Rajmahal and near a very fine ruin. This ruin had formerly been the residence of the Rajah of the place, but I fancy the encroachments of the Ganges gave him notice to quit, and in this country when a house is deserted it very soon moulders away. We went on shore to go over these ruins, and were very much gratified indeed. It was moonlight ere we left, and as we stood on a projecting part of the ruin which overhung the river, we might have exclaimed with the Poet:

To see Rajmahal aright,

etc., etc.★ After this burst of romance you will be shocked to hear that what can be made serviceable is used to keep coal in, this place being one of the dépôts for supplying the steam vessels as they go up!★★

★ She has in mind a couplet from Scott's *The Lay of the Last Minstrel:*
If thou wouldst view fair Melrose aright
Go visit it by the pale moonlight.

★★ Rajmahal had been capital of the province of Bengal under the Mughals and was renowned for its fine ruins, some of which

Christine took her baby on shore, to open its understanding, I suppose, and it was so disgustingly naughty it destroyed half my pleasure. I could not help thinking all the time how annoying it must be to my father to be doing his soldiering with two women and a squalling brat in his train and at his elbow!

Friday 23rd   Is a very bleak day in the way of news. Nothing occurred. We had fine views still of our mountains. We anchored off a most uninteresting piece of ground, which just did for the Hindoo cooking and for Henry to give his dog, Dart, a swim to shore and a walk along the bank; but it was a high jungle down to the water's edge and quite unfit for amusement. Something moreover had died hard bye, which caused a most dreadfully putrid smell, and we all went to bed uneasy in our minds, as the doctor assured us that it was a thing to produce cholera and that we ought to drop down out of the way of it; but we felt sure this would

---

incorporated marble, a material rare in Bengal. The decision to use a marble-lined hall as a coal dépôt for steamships stimulated a debate resembling the conflict between 'conservation' and 'development' of our own day, and which well illustrates how strong at this time were the dogma of progress and the belief in Western technology as its agent. 'While some persons consider the conversion of the marble hall into a dépôt for coals as a shocking desecration', wrote Emma Roberts, 'others are of opinion that the element of this new power, which is changing all the moral, political and physical relations of the world, and is working a revolution more stupendous and radical than any that history records, is well lodged in a palace. The hall, once filled with courtiers blazing in diamonds, now contains the true diamond; while the emblem of that astonishing power, whose gigantic resources it is impossible to calculate, lying at anchor under the buttresses of the ancient towers of Rajmahal, in the shape of a steam vessel, can scarcely fail to fill the contemplative mind with gorgeous visions of the future.' (Commentary by Emma Roberts in George Francis White's *Views in India*: London, 1838, p.13)

not be, because my father's sense of smelling is not acute, and although *we* were poisoned, *he* smelt nothing. There were moreover native boats anchored close to us, and they kept up an incessant noise either with some musical instrument or for the purpose of frightening away wild animals from cattle which were grazing in the neighbourhood. However, it was a cool night by comparison, and we are none the worse for either smells or noise. I sleep now in my day chemmy with a string round the bosom just to keep it on; neither upper nor under sheet, but I lie on what is called here a cold mat, a nice, smooth, slippery thing, which is cooler than anything else.

Saturday 24th   At noon today we passed some very picturesque rocks, which stand out of the river and are called the Colgong Rocks. There is a tremendous stream rushing between them and the mainland – as we know by experience, for our steamer was obliged here to let out her steam to take in coal from a boat. Unfortunately it overtook us at this point, and we rapidly went back. In due course we regained our lost position and anchored rather later than usual; but none of us went on shore. It was a very nice cool night.

Sunday 25th   At daylight this morning there was much firing amongst the gentlemen. The banks of the river were swarming with alligators, which they shot at every time a brute raised its head above the water; but it seemed to me both cruel and stupid sport, for they could not be taken. At eleven o'clock we anchored off a place called Baughelpore [Bhagalpur], famous for its manufacture of silk, of a very ugly texture but useful here and *very serviceable* in England, where it washes well and lasts for ever. John went on shore for letters.

We hoped to find some from England, but were disappointed. He was not satisfied with the reception he met with, for he had to walk a mile in the broiling sun, and the gentleman to whose house he went never asked him whether he would have a glass of wine. We have been much amused in the course of the day by the mode in which the natives convey their butter etc., etc. to market. They sit or hold on some buoyant thing and so float down the river, their heads merely appearing above the water with their merchandise tied to the end of a stick, which they hold up out of the water to preserve it; and thus they travel looking as comfortable as we should in our coach and four. We anchored late and off a place where there was no landing.

Wednesday 28th   We got on very well this morning from daybreak until ten o'clock, at which hour we found ourselves comfortably aground on a sandbank. We did not think much of this at the time, as we had been so often before. But alas! how little did we know what was before us, for we stuck on and stuck on, and although the crew of lascars and all our own servants worked very hard digging and pulling, in the water and out of the water, it was all of no use, and we never stirred until one o'clock on Thursday morning. It was the fault of the pilot, who was deceived in consequence of the rapid fall of the river in a few days. If you could see the pilot you would not be much surprised at his making the mistake, that is if we judge from outward appearance only. He was a black man with a turban on his head and a rag round his middle and looked anything but a philosopher. My father was very angry, for he thought the captains of both the steamer and flat acted stupidly and without energy or decision. It would be impossible for anyone who has not lived in this country at all to fancy anything like the noise and uproar that took place throughout the day. These people can never work without so much talk and screaming, and I do assure you at bedtime it was so dreadful I determined not to attempt to go to bed; nor did I until past twelve o'clock, but remained on deck. I then became so hungry I was driven down to seek for food, and having feasted well with John and Captain Campbell on cold duck and beer I went to bed and slept as well as a musquito would permit me. We were annoyed during the evening in a manner which baffles description by insects of all sorts and kinds, sizes and descriptions, which we attributed to the sandbank on which we were established, for we were a great distance from land on either side. There was one most alarming specie which flew in, of the cricket kind, but so large and so spiteful, and with such a pair of pincers. You may suppose what a size it must have been when I tell you we took it for a *bat*, and bore it quietly until we discovered what a monster it was. We then put an end to it, and I do nothing but regret I have not the means on board to preserve it.

Friday 30th   Today was an unpleasant day in some respects. It rained a good deal throughout the day, but then to counterbalance this evil it was very cool, almost cold. We amused ourselves for as long as we could see it with the ceremony of a Hindoo funeral. We saw the dead body lying on a thing like a ladder, wrapped up in a sheet, with its head close to the edge of the water so as to admit of its splashing over it occasionally. We saw the burning pile preparing, but got on too rapidly to see more. We passed the city of Patna, which extends for six miles along the banks of the river, but it is a dismal-looking place with very few good-looking houses. It is famous for its manufacture of wax candles and a cotton manufacture for table cloths, table napkins, towels etc.; very cheap and very useful in this country, where it is a crying sin to have damask. My father unfortunately brought out much of this, which the dobies have made mincemeat of. I have made him purchase table cloths of the Patna manufacture for common use, and he is going to do the same for the napkins. I hope you like this interesting bit of information. We anchored at sunset off a place at the extreme end of Patna called Bankipoor.

Saturday October 1st   At half-past eight o'clock this morning we all went on shore. There is a Mr Trotter who lives here. He is the opium man who has given E. Hodges his new occupation. He is an old and intimate friend of the W. Fanes. On all these accounts my father accepted his hospitable invitation to breakfast. We are so punctual, and the inhabitants, or European residents rather, so much the contrary, that instead of finding carriages ready at the appointed hour to convey us to Mr Trotter's house we had to wait half an hour at least before they came. There was fortunately a beautiful peepul tree, under which we all waited. At length Mr Trotter (who is the image of Mr Hodges) made his appearance with his conveyances, and we adjourned to his house. He was a particularly nice man, had a particularly nice house and gave us a particularly nice breakfast. We sat down about fifteen *livery*-looking beings, all men, and after breakfast I received a visit from a Mrs and Miss Tucker. The latter I had had the pleasure of seeing during the fashionable season at Calcutta, but not the mama, for she was sick. She has been lots of years in India, but looks as if death will not allow her to remain lots more. She looked like a dug-up corpse. We had a violent case of cholera on board yesterday. One of my brother's servants was seized with it. He is however about his work today, wonderful to relate. The doctor thought at one time that he must

126

die. He was so bad he could not swallow. We anchored in the afternoon off Dinapoor. Soon after, the return steamer from Allahabad passed us, performed a pretty revolution round us, took up some passengers and proceeded on its passage. We anchored just off Brigadier Beecher's bungalow, who is very civil to us and furnishes us with carriages to drive of an evening. We went this evening towards Patna. The country about here is just now much covered with Indian corn, and that part which is not is preparing for the cultivation of the poppy. This is the great opium district, and it is just on the opposite side of the river that E. Hodges is to settle. He is here just now, and goes to Muzzeffapur to his business at the end of the week.

Sunday 2nd   I got up at five o'clock this morning to go with my father and the two Henrys to church at the cantonments. The morning was so cold I was perished going to and also whilst at church. The clergyman was not a bad performer, but his sermon was not particularly edifying. We returned on board to bathe and to breakfast. Went on shore again to drive in the evening, and the Brigadier gave us a fête. There were three ladies besides ourselves. One was reckoned a beauty. She certainly was, compared with the other two; but in our sweet country, where beauty is a more common commodity, no one would have stopped his horse from a gallop to look at her. One other lady was a perfect monster, and if I had dared I could have behaved very ill on her account. She had a husband who was nearly as great a brute to look at as herself.

Monday 3rd   My father saw a portion of the troops at gun fire, or sunrise, this morning. I did not go because I am tired of military spectacles, and Christine did not go

127

because she thinks her baby better worth attending to than anything else. They all returned on board for breakfast, but after breakfast my father went on shore to hold a levée. In the evening we all went to drive and to walk over a practical farm in the neighbourhood, where you can replenish your stores with anything and everything. We purchased some delicious sausages. We took leave of Edward Hodges here. We returned on board to tea and invited our Captain to join us, who is such a vulgar man but who conducted himself with great propriety and enlightened all our minds with the history of indigo making, he having dabbled in it once himself. Played our casino, and went to bed.

Thursday 6th   Went on today but badly, in consequence of having wood fuel instead of coal. Wood does not generate sufficient steam, and the paddles instead of making twenty-seven revolutions in a given time made but nineteen. The consequence of this was that at four o'clock, upon our getting into a very strong current against us, we could not budge, but on the contrary went back; and after struggling until sunset we were obliged to anchor. The next morning, Friday 7th, we struggled from sunrise until eight trying to stem the stream, but all to no purpose, and were obliged to send to Buxar, eight miles, to desire coals might be sent to us. They came in due time, and at one o'clock the steam was got up and we again endeavoured to start; but it baffled even the coal steam and we were obliged to get fifty men, dandies as they are called [*dandi*-oarsman], to tow us. Our difficulty only lay in a space of a few hundred yards, and having conquered it we went on very well and arrived at about half-past five at Buxar. This place contains the stud for supplying the Bengal army with horses. The establishment contains about

7,000, and about 400 is the annual supply to the regiments.

Saturday 8th   At daylight this morning we went on shore to see the stud. Mr Chaplin would have been so delighted had he seen all we saw. The stables are so beautiful, and we saw about 400 horses and colts of two and three years old. After walking through their stables we saw 200 at a time let out loose into their paddocks, and you cannot imagine what a pretty thing it was to see their frolics. Altogether it was a very interesting exhibition. We returned on board to breakfast and bathe. We had two gentlemen to dine with us. One was Captain Mackenzie, the head manager of the stud – an ugly but good-natured man, who lost his wife three years ago and has never held up his head since. And no wonder, for in this country at an out-station a man must love his wife even if she were a very devil, and miss her when she dies. Fancy, here at Buxar there is but one lady. We had not the pleasure of seeing her, but if she is agreeable in proportion to her husband, one Captain Spottiswood, she must be a neat article. Captain Mackenzie has three daughters on the high seas about to join him. God help them! Their only associates will be this man and his wife, the M.D. of the station, the veterinary surgeon – and I believe these are all. What would induce me I wonder to marry and settle in India! At Buxar we received English newspapers and letters, and yours of April and May I have to offer you my very best thanks for. I am glad you liked my bit of scandal. I wonder what it was! I like your method of communicating yours, and shall adopt it for the future if I should have any to tell you; but having left the city we shall now only associate with the virtuous and pure minded! We are now at Ghazepoor [Ghazipur], from whence this is

129

to be despatched, so I will now conclude it. I am very apprehensive that my journals now will be both longer and more frequent than you will approve of. With love to all, believe me dear Mrs Chaplin,

Yours very affectionately,

I. Fane.

IX

[The packet covering the period from October 9th to November 7th is missing. To supply the gap an extract from Isabella's journal is now inserted.]

Sunday 9th   We arrived at about four o'clock at Gazhepore [Ghazipur]. This is by far the prettiest station we have yet seen. In the evening we went on shore to Mr Trotter's house. He is brother to Mr Trotter at Bankipore. He took us a drive. Lord Cornwallis is buried here; at least, he died here and there is a monument to him. A dinner party in the evening. There is another portion of the stud here, and the town is famous for its manufacture of rosewater.

Wednesday 12th   At five o'clock came in sight of Benares, a most striking city, full of ghauts [*ghat*, landing place, ford] temples, etc., etc., which extend along the banks of the river and form a beautiful amphitheatre. We sailed along it and returned again to our anchoring ground to have a view of the city.

Thursday 13th   My father saw the troops in the morning, officers on board the flat in the day. Captain Anson visited us here. We had merchants on board to

131

exhibit the beautiful gold and silver fabrics for which this place is famous. The principal merchant here is one Runjeet Singh. In the evening we mounted elephants to lionize the city and were much amused at all we saw. The streets are so narrow that into many not even a horse can go. Those we went down just held an elephant. The streets were crowded with inhabitants, but no wonder, for the population amounts to 600,000. We returned to our Noah's ark in the Rajah's barge, a very novel machine, but very comfortable.

Friday 14th   At half past eleven a.m. we left Benares. As we passed the Rajah's residence he fired a salute. We anchored about five o'clock at a place called Sooltanpoor [Sultanpur], which is a military station. A regiment of native cavalry is quartered here. My father etc. went on shore to see the stables, and Christine and I, Captain Campbell and Dr. Wood took a small walk to the cantonments.

Saturday 15th   My father inspected the cavalry at sunrise. After he again came on board we proceeded to a place called Chunar, about eight miles further on, where we anchored for the rest of the day. There is a fort here, very commandingly situated. It is garrisoned by invalids. We all went on shore and over the fort. Saw the armoury and some prisoners who are confined there for murder. Their term of imprisonment is to be ten years, five only having expired. We took a short drive after we had seen what there was to see and returned on board to tea.

Sunday 16th   Left Chunar under a salute from the battery at sunrise. Anchored at Mirzapore, went on shore and had a very nice drive in one Dr Campbell's carriage. Mirzapore is famous for its manufacture of carpets. It is situated on the top of a high bank.

Monday 17th   We stuck this morning for two hours in rather an awkward place, with rocks on one side, a sand bank and a strong current besides. We got off without damage and anchored at sunset off no particular place.

Wednesday 19th   Stuck twice but reached Allahabad that afternoon. Drove out to see the station, which is extensive and pretty and dined a nice family party.

Thursday 20th   Visitors. A drive, dinner *en famille* and cards.

Friday 21st   A station ball, which proved a great nuisance to us all.

Saturday 22nd   A dinner party not more amusing than the ball.

Sunday 23rd   Went to church twice. Mr Pratt, the clergyman, was the best preacher and reader I have heard in India.

Monday 24th   I took a ride in the evening on my own horse, with Marc.

Tuesday 25th   The usual routine.

Wednesday 26th   A reunion ball. I rode with Caroline and was shook to a mummy, and did not attend.

Thursday 27th   Mr Fane got a fall from his horse this evening and hurt his leg.

Friday 28th   Mrs Fane's ball.

Saturday 29th   A dinner at Mr Turnbull's.

Sunday 30th   Church. Nothing in the evening. Played Dr Wood a trick.

Monday 31st   Amateur play. Very stupid.

Tuesday November 1st   We gave an entertainment in our tent which went off very well.

Wednesday 2nd   This afternoon we visited the Byza Beea, or widow of Sindia. We had a stupid visit and a bad interpretess, one Mrs Parks.★ The gentlemen dined at a grand entertainment given by the station to His Excellency.

★ The Baiza Bai was the widow of Maharaja Daulat Rao Sindia, the Mahratta ruler of Gwalior. After acting as regent for nine years after her husband's death she had been ousted by a palace revolt and forced to seek asylum in British territory. Mrs Fanny Parks recorded several meetings with her, including that mentioned here, in her book *Wanderings of a Pilgrim in Search of the Picturesque* (London, 1850)

134

Thursday 3rd   A lady dinner party in camp.

Friday 4th   Mr Lowther's fancy sale.

Saturday 5th   A man dinner party in camp.

Sunday 6th   Church and nothing.

Monday 7th   Visitors and bustle.

Tuesday 8th   This morning at daylight His Excellency left Allahabad. Caroline, Marc, Henry Fane and myself did not join the camp until the evening. It halted eight miles from Allahabad. Things were not quite comfortably arranged, but still for young beginners they were better than could have been expected.

X

My Dear Mrs Chaplin,

We left Allahabad with great regret on Tuesday November 8th. My father, as he likes to do things in an exact manner, in order to arrange himself went to sleep in his tent at the camp after his rubber of whist on Monday evening. So he started at six o'clock on Tuesday morning on an elephant, attended by all his suite save M. Beresford and Henry Fane. Because we are beginners in the marching way, he determined that the first two days' march should be short, so as not to fatigue either the two– or four-footed beasts. This being the case, I adopted a plan suggested by Mrs W. Fane, and as the camp marched only eight miles from Allahabad, I was driven to it by Henry Fane in John's buggy in the evening. Carry had a wedding to attend, in the capacity of bridesmaid, in the morning at nine o'clock, so her mama drove us in her carriage four miles of the road. She then finished her journey on horseback chaperoned by Marc, whilst H. and I proceeded in the way I have above mentioned. The road was said to be very good. It was about two feet deep in sand the whole way, and the dust was indescribable. We reached the camp about six o'clock, had tea, and afterwards did not know in the least what to do with ourselves. Most of the others were in bed by eight o'clock; but Carry and I found a pack of cards and sat down and played écarté. You have no idea of the fuss and bother there has been about the conveyance of my goods. I am nobody's property but my father's, and of course I could not plague him about trumpery. Henry ought to have looked after me, but he thinks of no one but his wife, dog and child, so a day or two before starting I found I was without the necessaries of a camp life. I thought I should have gone distracted. I had no camels allotted to me, and no carts, because people had helped themselves. However, I am all right now, so never mind.

Wednesday 9th   We had only a march of eight miles to do today, so we were drest and ready to start at six o'clock. Our elephants awaited us outside our tent door; so Carry and I, Marc and my maid and my little dog mounted on one, and my father and his Jemidar in solitary grandeur on another, and off we started. It was not quite dark. Our elephant is a particularly easy one when weighted; but Car and Colonel Beresford get off and ride half the distance, and then I am much more shaken. I get into the palanquin now when they go, which I think such a delicious mode of conveyance, and I take a very pleasant nap therein. After we get in, we wash (a very necessary operation, I assure you), go to breakfast, receive visitors (for there are several ladies in the camp), and dine at half-past two. This evening several of us rode and explored the country and went into a village. The former is frightful but well-cultivated; the latter was wretched-looking and the streets so narrow there was barely room for our horses. We returned home to tea, played at cards and went to bed.

Thursday 10th & Friday 11th   We did just the same, except that the evening of the former day I went with John, Carry and Marc to see the elephants and camels etc., etc. fed; and on the evening of the latter I rode with my father to see what was to be seen within riding distance. This consisted of a village, a fort, and some very extraordinary ground, caused by the rain during the rainy season, which had broken it up in a very wonderful manner. I have got such a horrid cold and cough, the common seasoning to those who first begin a camp life; and yet the nights are not so cold as I had hoped and expected. I can bear only a blanket yet. In the daytime it is very hot, but we have a punkah in our tent.

Saturday 12th   We halted this morning in a beautiful grove. The street formed by the tents is a beautiful avenue. If a tree stands in the way when the camp is forming, it is instantly chopped down. The grove is full of green parrots. They make a great screaming and put me in mind of my poor talking polly, who died in Calcutta. A tiger, report says, lives sixteen miles from hence, and it has eaten three people; but in consequence of this latter circumstance no one believes the existence of the beast. Captain Campbell, being an old Indian, and his liver being shorn of its fair proportions, braves the midday sun. He went out shooting yesterday on an elephant, and brought home a few quail and one black partridge; the sport at present is not worth seeking. I did not stir out this evening, but nursed my cold and read *Ellen Wareham* [unidentified], or rather had it read to me. It is a very pretty tale, and rather touching. I have not a bit of voice left.

Sunday 13th   We did not stir today, and did we not enjoy lying in bed until eight o'clock! Marc Beresford read the morning service in our dining tent to such as chose to form a congregation. He performed admirably, excepting that he read the 18th instead of the 13th day of the month, prayed for George instead of William and read a wrong chapter in the Bible because the right one was too long. We had one timid man to dinner. My father when he sat down had two or three violent twinges in his ancle, which alarmed him much, as he apprehended gout; but it turned out nothing. He rode in the evening, as did Carry etc., etc.; I did nothing but staid in my tent to nurse my cold and have the last Calcutta newspaper read to me.

Monday 14th   My cold being bad, I went the whole of this morning's march in the palanquin. I merely turned out of bed, put on a cloak etc., took my pillows and lay down and finished my sleep there just as comfortably as if I had been in bed. I have already got used to the change of bearers, and it does not disturb me. We halted in another nice grove. Our march was thirteen miles.

Tuesday 15th   I am sorry to say that my father's twinges in his ancle had been so bad all Monday night that he did not sleep a wink; but still it was not confirmed gout. He went in his palanquin carriage instead of on his elephant or on horseback, and arrived at our station not at all the worse for the journey. He instantly set to work with polcycum (I don't know how to spell it) [?] and he felt much less of the pain throughout the day; so we live in hopes it will not turn to gout but turn out an accidental pain. We halted today at the civil station of Futtipore [Fatehpur], on a hot exposed piece of ground with a hideous gigantic idol at the end of our street. The civilians, six in number, came to *boo* to my father. In the evening Henry Fane and I rode into the city to see what was to be seen, which amounted to nothing but some mosques. All mosques are so much alike that, excepting some are larger than others, having seen one you have seen them all, I think.

Wednesday 16th   My father slept well last night, but prudently travelled the same way this morning. He has got on a boot, and flatters himself it will terminate favourably. It would be a dreadful calamity if he fell sick now, within two days of Cawnpore [Kanpur], where such grand doings are to take place and so many troops are awaiting him. We went this morning to return the ladies' visits, and a droll picture we must have made. I was in my tonjohn, a thing like the body of a buggy but borne on men's shoulders; Christine had a China umbrella over her head; Car an English one; but the oddest part of all was that a man followed us with three chairs, for in camp everyone brings a chair with him wherever he goes. The sun was dreadful, and we have all got pains in our heads in consequence. I rode with Marc in the evening, and he talked so much, and cried, about poor Mrs Beresford. Poor man. After her death he washed her, and put her grave clothes on her, and put her himself in her coffin. The malady she died of was of a nature which made her a far from pleasing sight and, it appears, this impression he cannot get from his mind for an instant when alone. It troubles him much.

Thursday 17th   I am sorry to say my father had another bad night on Wednesday, from the pain in his foot. It affects his spirits more much than his body; he is under such alarm that he should be disabled whilst at Cawnpore. He travelled well in his carriage and four, and was much better throughout the day. We had a lady – Mrs Torrens,★ a very nice lady – who brought her

★ Wife of Colonel R. Torrens. See p. 101.

work and spent the morning with us. John and Captain Campbell went out shooting and were rewarded for the risk they ran of frizzling their livers by killing a wild pig, a nilghai (a species of deer), some partridges and some quail. In the evening I rode out with Henry Fane, and we were much pleased with having fallen in with a betrothement. The ceremony took place in a grove. The betrothed were two children drest very fine, and they looked about nine years old. There was much wild music, a nautch girl, and a great deal of tumult. There was besides a procession, amongst which shone conspicuous a wooden elephant drawn on wheels and a horse in the same style, besides various other curious things.

Saturday 19th   This morning we had only a march of eight miles to do before we reached the station of Cawnpore, so we were able to indulge in bed until six o'clock. My poor father, added to his other calamity of the pain in his foot, has a bad boil on a most inconvenient part of his body. Notwithstanding this, he felt himself compelled to mount his horse to ride into camp with the military authorities of the place. He got through it pretty well. This is a large station, seven miles in extent. The country is frightful and the dust indescribable. I am so disappointed in it, for I had made up my mind to find it a town, with plenty of streets and three-storied houses, instead of which it consists of detached bungalows. But it contains much military; amongst them a lancer regiment who think themselves fine little fellows. This is the most scandalous, gossiping station in all India, which if you knew but all, is saying much in its favour. The two great people are Brigadier Churchill★ and General

---

★ At this stage Commandant at Kanpur. Shortly after he was promoted Major-General and appointed Quartermaster-General, Bengal Army.

141

Stevenson. The former is a terrible man, and does everything that is bad. His wife was a very handsome woman, but her *reputation* is not as pure as un-sunned snow. Whether this is just or not I cannot say. She is a most impudent-looking woman, rouged to a vermilion colour. They have an only child, a daughter, an exceedingly pretty girl, and, with such parents, in a very good *moral* school. The other man has a daughter, who presides over his establishment, with Malay blood in her veins. She is a handsome-looking *young* lady, of about *my* time of life, but she provokes me because of her style of head. She wears two long love locks coaxed out of her back hair, which recline on her scraggy bosom; then she tucks up a curl here, and lets down another there, and so on. Her reputation is unfair also; but we are obliged to wink at all this and be most polite. However, the world is very scandalous, and in excuse for the first a faithless husband goes far. As for the second, she was jilted by Captain Mundy! Of course, all sorts of things are done by way of entertaining us, so on Monday we sat down about sixty to dinner at General Stevenson's. I thought it never would have ended; but as soon as it did, which was about half-past nine, my father came home, for his boil made sitting very unpleasant. Very happy we females were to get away also. There was dancing in the evening, for which the A.D.C.s waited, but poor Carry lost this. Fortunately she does not care for society.

The following morning my father had the grand review, the anticipation of which had brought so many from various places. I believe the spectacle, to those who understand such matters, was but indifferent; for my part I am ashamed to say I understand so little of them that I don't take much interest. Therefore by nine o'clock, the time it all ended, I had become very hot and bored and should have been very glad to return to camp had it not been for an ugly, vulgar woman whose husband had done us a civility the day before. We were compelled to do one in return, by asking this thing and a boy about five years old to breakfast, and she stood very much in the way of our comfort. Fortunately she went away soon after, so we had not much in fact to bear or forbear. My father, poor man, felt so relieved when this was over. He got through it well, considering his unfortunate state. I am sorry to say the shooting pain in his foot still continues at intervals, although nothing comes of it whatever, neither swelling nor inflammation; nor does his health seem to suffer in the least. There were between five and six thousand men reviewed, and lots of artillery, both horse and bullock. Our party were mounted on three elephants, who stood all the firing very valiantly and showed no other signs of annoyance than trumpeting and wheeling short round. They ought not to have done even this, for they are all famous tiger-hunting elephants. One has a broken tail, and several lumps and bumps from their claws, etc. to prove the truth of the mahout's statement. We returned some visits in the course of the morning, and at night went to an amateur play. The piece was *The Floating Beacon* [by Edward Fitzball]. I am ashamed to say I was not so much bored as I had been on a similar occasion at Allahabad. It was bad enough; but my father, whose mind is greater than mine, was completely bored. We did not stay to the end; only to the end of the first piece. It was a dirty little house, and so cold.

Wednesday 23rd   My father had a levée this morning, and in the evening himself and staff dined at a great feast given to him by the military and civil of the station. It was unanimously agreed to be an exceeding gentlemanly and well-managed thing, and would have been quite perfect, only the gentlemen of the artillery chose to resent something my father had done about a Colonel

Faithfull, and had the good taste not to join the party. We ladies dined at home and had Marc and Henry to take care of us. The former does not go into society; the latter is sorely afflicted just now with a malady common to this country, called ringworm. It is not in his head, but in his joints, and is exceedingly painful and troublesome; but the doctors say it is a sign of health.

Thursday 24th   No one comes to call upon us. I daresay the ladies are sulky about something; goodness knows what. It is our gain. We all rode out. There was a large military dinner given by my father, so we ladies, Marc, Henry and Captain Anson had tea and cards in our own tents.

Friday 25th   At twelve o'clock today we had to attend a fancy sale, the benefits of which were for an orphan asylum that receives and educates a lot of little children bought by individuals during a famine which took place in Bundelcund [Bundelkhand] about three years ago. The little children are brought up to be ayahs [nursemaids]. They are capable of learning much that is useful, but it is found *impossible* to break them of the innate love for *lying* which all natives possess. You cannot fancy the barefaced manner in which they do this; but then, wretched creatures, they look upon it as a feather in their caps instead of a sin. About the sale: it was infinitely worse than the one at Allahabad. Even so, my father subscribed £20 to it, so we were not compelled to purchase much, nor did we stay long. There blew today a little wind, which gave us a specimen of the real charms of Cawnpore. The dust was so dreadful that we could not see a yard before us; but we were assured that this was a trifle to what it is during the hot winds in the month of May, when from the darkness occasioned by the dust people are obliged to light candles at noonday.

Sunday 27th   Divine service was performed in the lancer riding school, for Cawnpore, to its shame be it told, does not contain a church. It was a very pretty sight to the uninitiated. Carry and I were in a gallery and the *coup d'oeil* from it was very striking. A great panic was caused by a dog, which had followed its master into the place and which had excited my admiration by its orderly conduct, being seized with a fit. After struggling and kicking and eating the dust for some minutes it got up and staggered in amongst the soldiers. Hydrophobia was the first thing that occurred to their minds, and with one accord numbers sprang upon the benches. At length one valiant soldier stepped out, took the poor dog by the scruff of the neck and dragged him out, and quiet was restored. The clergyman did the duty well, but the sermon I could not benefit by, I lost so much of it from the size of the room.

Monday 28th   There was a very pretty review this morning, but we were told it was not to be interesting, so we did not get up to see it. We were very provoked about it, for there was so much row from artillery etc., our tents shook, and sleep was out of the question, so we might as well have been up. The only thing which reconciled us to our misfortune was that the morning was absolutely perishing, and we were so snug in bed. The next event which happened today was my being put into a towering passion by a letter which I received from Mrs W. Fane and one which I read from Mr Fane to Marc, by which it appeared that that nasty girl Miss Dickie had written a great pack of *lies* from hence about us, and made great mischief and drawn down the indignation of both upon us when we did not in the least deserve it. I think her odious. I did before this happened, but now my admiration is not increased. She is such a gossip and toadies Mrs Fane in such a manner, and bullies Car. She is old and ugly and sick-looking, with black teeth and a bad complexion. There was another great military dinner given to my father, and there was also a grand station ball to which we all went. It was exceedingly well attended, and we all danced a great deal. Carry looked very nice in a tulle dress she brought from England, and a wealth of flowers in her hair. We were not home until two o'clock. I had that morning received your packet of July. In this you talk of my grandeur, and the airs I shall give myself when I return. I thought of you on this occasion much, I was *so* great. I was met at the door by the two greatest men at the station and marched into the room supported by them. One was seventy, the other a hundred I believe. Well, when it was supper time, no one could go till I did, and the great man and an A.D.C. came and fetched me. But indeed, dear Mrs Chaplin, this will not do me any harm; I don't dislike my position, but I shall feel my utter insignificance again on my return to my native land, and act as before.

Tuesday 29th   At twelve o'clock today we all went to the riding school to see a picked set of lancers go through the lance exercise. I had never seen anything of the sort before, and was very well amused. It is a very pretty exhibition. I took such a nice drive in the buggy with Marc this evening. The rest rode. We saw more of Cawnpore in this drive than we have yet done. It is astonishing to see with what force the rain must come down. The face of the country all about this station is torn up until deep ravines are formed, and it gives it a very singular appearance. There is not a bit of anything either pretty or picturesque. My father had a large military and civil dinner, and we had a snug evening in his tent to ourselves.

Thursday December 1st   This morning at sunrise there was a grand cavalry review. Carry and I attended on our elephant. The cold was terrific and we went in consequence more as a duty than from pleasure, and with our minds impressed with the folly of it, as ladies never see anything on these occasions. Our virtue was rewarded, for we saw everything beautifully. We followed my father and staff closely. Our elephants behaved most heroically, and although there was much cannonading, and we were close to it, they did nothing but trumpet. There was another small dinner party this evening and Mrs Torrens, the wife of the King's Adjutant-General, gave us tea and cards and music in her tent. If you could but know what we now endure night and morning from cold.

Friday 2nd   At four o'clock this afternoon a party of us went on elephants to see some Mahrattas perform their feats of horsemanship. They used formerly to be famous in this way, but times are strangely altered and we were much disappointed at the exhibition. Their horses are wonderfully broken, and they pull them up like a shot from their quickest pace. They wheel them round and round also in a beautiful manner. Their chief feat, which is firing with a matchlock at a wine bottle loaded with ball, with their horses at top speed, they all failed in. They never touched the bottle once. The chief man was much distressed at this, and in excuse said they had not tried it for eight years. We in excuse for them observed that the dust was great. We dined with

Brigadier Churchill; a large party and tedious repast. Dancing was the order of the evening, which answered very well, and all seemed much amused. The band of the 16th Lancers played, which is a very good one. My father played whist, and we were not home until one o'clock. Carry danced plenty, and seemed to enjoy herself. At dinner she looked miserable. She sat between General Stevenson, aged seventy, and Colonel Kennedy, about the same time of life. Each smoked a hookah and was altogether pleasant.

Saturday 3rd   I have nothing to tell about, therefore I may here say, what I forgot to say before, that our new Persian Interpreter [Captain Hay] is come. He joined us here, at Cawnpore. He is young, ugly and shy; an excellent Persian scholar, and a quiet, well-behaved man. We leave Cawnpore on Thursday next, the 8th. Carry leaves us on Wednesday morning with Colonel Beresford, who has kindly undertaken to escort her all the way back to Allahabad and to overtake us in the best and most expeditious manner – which will not be an affair of much difficulty by forced marches. We are very tired of the dust and smoke of this place. Adieu, dear Mrs Chaplin. Give my affectionate love to all to whom it will be acceptable and believe me

Yours very affectionately,

I. Fane.

XI

My Dear Mrs Chaplin,

We left Cawnpore on the 8th at half-past six in the morning. But before I talk of ourselves, I must just mention that Carry left us the morning before, at four o'clock, accompanied by Marc. We all missed her very much, for although she is not more lively than when she left England, she is so gentle and amiable that one cannot do otherwise than like her. Marc accompanied her all the way to Allahabad. We were all rejoiced at this, not only for *her* sake, but also for our own, or I may say *particularly* for *my* own, for that *very detestable* creature, Miss Dickie, had gossiped and made such mischief with the W. Fanes that we, and I, had placed ourselves in his hands to make a defence. I never saw so detestable a creature; the most arrant gossip the world ever produced, and *such* a *toady*. The indignation I feel at one's relations listening to a *beast* of that sort makes my blood boil. *I* have particular reason to be furious with her, for she hated me and I was the chief sufferer from her malicious tongue. I abhorred her from the moment I saw her, and as I cannot humbug I could not but treat her with the contempt I thought she deserved. I am afraid Marc has not done any good, for both Mr and Mrs Fane are determined to love her on and believe what she says, even though it be to the prejudice of their child. But I won't say more about her, for she is not worth it. His Excellency's exit from Cawnpore was a very pretty sight. All the military big-wigs of the place came to our camp with loads of the 16th Lancers, and these, with all his own staff and his own escort etc., etc., formed an exceedingly pretty *coup d'oeil*. They went with him about three miles, or clear of the cantonments, where I was awaiting him in the carriage equipped for riding.

Saturday 10th   My father and all our agents went out shooting at about eleven o'clock and staid until four. They were rewarded by a medley bag of game, consisting of partridge, hare and peacock. The two former are very tasteless in this country; the latter only fit for mulligatawny soup, unless the bird is quite young; then they say it is good.

Sunday 11th   We halted and indulged in bed until eight o'clock. No divine service, for Marc was away and my father did not think any of the rest of our men grave enough. I rode out in the evening with my father and Henry Fane, and we explored the neighbourhood. We found the land highly and most industriously cultivated and irrigated. It was a delightfully cool evening, and we enjoyed our ride very much. Great events happened in camp. An unfortunate servant injured himself so much from gunpowder our doctor was obliged to cut off his arm. A widow woman's only child was carried off by a wolf, and a camel tumbled down and broke its leg and was obliged to be shot.

Tuesday 13th   My birthday, but I did not mention it to anyone, because I am now arrived at a *shameful* age! I travelled as usual on my elephant half the march, and was so completely knocked up by it that I have come to the resolution to travel no more in this way, excepting on extraordinary occasions. We encamped today in a beautiful grove; it was the prettiest spot we have yet pitched in. About two miles from our camp were some beautiful ruins of the ancient city of Kanoge [Kanauj]. We rode to see them in the evening and were well rewarded. There was an exceedingly pretty Hindoo temple, as well as a Mohomedan mosque, both in ruins but both beautifully situated. The ruins extend altogether about seven miles. We had a guide with us and wandered about as long as the light would permit. We then returned to camp by a new road, and one that was very picturesque. The ground was much broken, there were many trees, and jackals crossed our path. My maid is very ill with a nervous fever, but she is not bad enough to be laid up. Indeed if she was, wretched woman, she could not. However, a march is not the best time for sickness, and I find it very inconvenient. I find her a most useful servant, and I have not the slightest trouble, she is so quick and clear-headed. She is engaged to be married to Lord Auckland's gentleman. Have I ever before mentioned that a march and a camp are famous for the robberies that take place? A great many have happened with us, and fancy how expert the robbers must be. Last night a gentleman, a Mr Armstrong, who commands or who belongs to the infantry escort, when he went to bed, in order to keep his clothes safe took them to bed with him; but, notwithstanding the precaution, when he awoke they were all gone. As they took his only blue undress military coat, he was seen on the march reduced to a white linen jacket. My father and I are quite safe and may leave anything about, for we are surrounded by a cloth wall and have many sentries to guard our tent.

Friday 16th   This morning we reached a place called Futtehgurh [Fatehgarh], where we halt for three days. It is a large dusty station, and contains troops and civilians and very nice European residences. Some of the ladies and gentlemen came to call upon us – one very pretty woman and one great fat vulgar ditto, with a husband who was perfectly insane on philosophy and who talked in so incoherent a manner that I got hot all over with pure fright. We have got into a horrible scrape about the wife of the colonel commanding here, about whom we were told all sorts of improper tales, *viz* that she was as black as my shoe and that she had lived for five years with this man before he married her. We were informed she meant to call, and were told we ought not to receive her. She did call, and we acted as directed. It afterwards came out she was received by all the ladies of the station, although the tongue of slander did talk of her. Upon finding out all this, I took the most ladylike and proper manner of retrieving my error, *viz* by writing her a very civil note, besides desiring a message to be given to her husband. Our not seeing her was put upon fatigue after our march. They have behaved like vulgarians and have taken no notice of either note or civil message, so they are at liberty after this display of bad taste to think of us as they like. My father had a levée and a durbar. We rode out in the evening, lost our way and were perished with the cold. We dined at six, and had an intimate or two from the camp. Had whist and a round game till bed time.

Saturday 17th   My father saw the troops here this morning and was much dissatisfied with them. The colonel (my friend Colonel Cooper) was so alarmed that after the inspection was over he was taken suddenly ill. My father and staff went to breakfast with the great man of the place, the Hakim Mehdie. He is a very good sort of old man, and was prime minister to the King of Oudh. You can read of him in Captain Mundy's travels.* I find Christine and I were expected. I would have given anything to have gone, it would have been an era in one's life! The breakfast was very good; plenty of dishes in which garlic was the predominant ingredient, but plenty of good tea and of good coffee also. It was dull, my father said; but of course where people hold converse through another it cannot be otherwise. Henry Fane had a very good breakfast; he acknowledges to have eaten six eggs! Christine and I spent such an idle day, with box wallahs [pedlars] who had very good Europe goods. Then at four o'clock the adopted son of the Hakim had a cheetah hunt an antelope for us. It was very cruel sport, for the poor antelope had such unfair play shewn him that the cheetah was upon him the very instant they were both set loose, and he was killed in about a minute. They are both beautiful animals. The cheetah is like a small tiger. I went on my elephant and was sorry not to have gone on my horse, but I thought it would have been like a fox hunt, with much galloping, which I did not think would suit my old hack. My father entertained the *he's* of the station, and we had a snug party of our own.

Sunday 18th There is a church here to which we went, my father and I, etc. The service was very tolerably done. After church Christine and I and some of our men went to see and hear the philosophy of that mad doctor I mentioned. We were exceedingly entertained and awestruck with the extraordinary mixture of cleverness and madness which he displayed. He has discovered that glass, which is a non-conductor in

---

* Oudh was a British protectorate in the central Ganges valley. The *Hakim* (physician) Mehdi Ali Khan was minister 1830–32 and again for six months before his death in 1837. He earned the approval of the British by his efforts to reform the government.

153

England, is here quite the reverse, which he proved to us in a number of curious ways; but what struck us with the most astonishment was his being able to move a bar of wood, about five feet long and about four inches in the diameter, with an eau-de-cologne bottle which was previously rubbed with a bit of silk. This bar of wood was supported on a pivot, which rested on a platform supported on bottles. I assure you he was most amusing, and very complimentary, for he dated these discoveries from my father's arrival in India. My father went this afternoon to return the visit of the great man who called upon him, *viz* the Rajah of Furrackabad [Farakhabad]. They all seem to have been very much amused with their visit. It was five miles from the camp. The man's house, they say, was finely situated. It was large, but contained nothing remarkable inside. What amused them most of all was the man's guard of honour, which was composed of so ragamuffin a crew that nothing but Colonel Evans's army could come up to it.

Tuesday 20th　　My father went out shooting this morning at dawn of day and killed some hares, some quail, some partridge and a peacock, which we had made into a spiced pie. The game of this country is much better so manufactured than plainly roast. We had a man or two to dinner, and whist, and a round game for us babies. We played at speculation, which forcibly recalled to my mind the charming noise we used to make at Blankney on similar occasions. In this we made so much, particularly Christine and I, that my father was ashamed of us and declared he would not play at whist for us. I do not believe I have ever mentioned that we have a little stove, like those that many shops own, in which we have a blazing fire every night. A piece of our great large tent is partitioned off, and you cannot think how snug we are of an evening.

Wednesday 21st   Today we reached a small station called Mynpoorie [Mainpuri]. The road to it was so infamous we were nearly jolted out of the buggy. A native regiment is stationed here, and some civilians, forming a society of *three* ladies, one of whom is so poor, and has her quiver so full of bairns, or *babas* as they are here called, that she cannot stir from home; so the Mynpoorie *monde* is reduced to two! The head lady of the station called upon us, and we found her ladylike and talkative. At four o'clock my father inspected the handful of troops. Christine and I, and Captain Campbell, went on an elephant to see it. I believe we must gave got tipsy at dinner, we were all three much too frolicsome for our years. The poor dear blackies acquitted themselves beautifully, and the Europe major who commanded them made us laugh immoderately, he had such an odd noddle of the head every time he gave the word of command. I dare say you are surprised and disappointed that I never mention the face of the country to you, but you must understand there is nothing to mention. You cannot conceive anything so flat and hideous as every particle we have up to this time travelled through. The villages even are not worthy of mention, but consist of the most wretched-looking mud huts, worse even, they say, than an Irish cabin, all huddled together and most unpicturesque.

Friday 23rd   I went in my usual way, palanquin and buggy. The road was shocking. We have no regular made road now to go upon, but cross commons and ravines and anything and everything as it comes. My father and some of his people went out gunning after breakfast, but had no sport. He shot a jackal. Some rain fell this morning, which is a working for a torrent we are to have on or about Christmas Day; but it will only be for a day or so if it does come.

Saturday 24th We had only about eight miles to march today, so we were not roused out of bed until six o'clock. Our tents were pitched near the town of Shekoabad [Shikohabad]. At one end of our camp were such high sand hills that by comparison we considered ourselves in a mountainous country. In the evening I rode with my father, etc. through the town. In England it would be denominated a village. It contained one long narrow street just wide enough to contain one horse. The houses were of mud, the inhabitants very numerous and the chief article of commerce seemed to be cotton, from the cotton plant, which is much used in this country in the same manner that wadding is used in ours. We all have silk quilts for our beds with it, and they are so warm and light. Gowns, dressing gowns, cloaks, etc., etc. are all made comfortable by this means, and now that we are all dying of the cold we find it indispensable. We had some of the young men belonging to the escort to dinner, and mustered two rubbers of casino.

Sunday 25th Christmas Day! How unlike one in England. It was dreadfully cold, but no snow, nor anything to put one in mind of our own dear homes and friends and the delightful family assemblages that take place at Fulbeck on this day. We always halt of a Sunday to refresh man and beast and, I am happy to say, for the sake of example my father is properly particular about its observance. He will not allow the gents of his staff to go out shooting on this day, which they would do if he did not prevent it, and I understand it has not been the custom before to have prayers read in the Commander-in-Chief's camp; so you see your respected brother is about to turn saint. Marc read the service to a very fair congregation. Poor fellow, he did not like doing it today, for every *marked* day recalls the past more vividly and he deeply feels his loss. We rode this evening to see a garden we spied out in our ride of last evening, which was attached to a native residence of commanding appearance at the end of the town of Shekoabad. We ascertained that the house belonged to a native who, in consequence of not being able to pay his due to John Company, was obliged to let all go to rack and ruin. The garden must have been very pretty when in order; but we experienced much disappointment, for it contained nothing but marigolds and Prince of Wales feather. We explored our way to it, and travelled over a country richly cultivated in corn, which looked most flourishing from artificial irrigation. We also went through very fine fields of castor-oil plant and capsicums. Castor-oil fields are as common as turnip fields in England. Because of its being Christmas Day we had a huge dinner party and sat down about twenty-three.

We have one young lady attached to our camp who had just arrived from England when her parents started to accompany my father in his military capacity of Judge-Advocate General; but she is too insipid, ugly and vulgar even for John, so at present John is without one string to his bow. I rejoice at this, for I have become impatient at his conduct, and cannot bear to see him sacrificing the feelings, one after another, of simple young girls, just for his own amusement. Four horrid instances of the sort have come before me since he began his Indian career, besides other female villainy. There is a girl who will join us at Meerut, about whom I have made up my mind he must get into trouble. Her father succeeds a man who resigned his situation at Cawnpore on account of his health. She is beautiful, only eighteen, an immense flirt and conscious of her powers. John will never be able to resist a great flirtation with her, I anticipate – meaning nothing, for she cannot be rich enough for him. Her father owes *mints* more than he can ever pay, and both parents' characters are at a low ebb. I think I have mentioned them in a previous series of journal.★ Their name is Churchill. I trust I may find myself mistaken about this business, but I confess I have my doubts.

Tuesday 27th   Another place for tombs. After breakfast Dr Wood, H. Fane, Captain Hay and myself set out to look at them. They were in a very dilapidated state, but must have been handsome in the days of their youth. The walls truly showed how many Europeans had visited them, for they were covered from top to bottom with names deeply carved. In my opinion those who were guilty of the offence were worthy of punishment.

Wednesday 28th   This morning we reached the famed city of Agra. The roads into it were dreadful, but their badness this morning was a mercy so far as Marc and I were concerned. He had a horse in the carriage that did its utmost to run away, but fortunately the sand was so deep he could only manage a few yards. My father was met by the military, and so escorted into the fort. Wretched man, he has got another bad boil in the same inconvenient place, which is again most annoying, for he has troops to see here, and must be on horseback. Upon his arrival at camp the European troops, or a part

★ See pp. 141–2.

of them, were assembled to meet him, and the band struck up *God Save the King*. Sir C. Metcalfe is Lieutenant-Governor of the Western Provinces, and resides here; so at three o'clock my father went in state to pay him a visit and found him fat and sleek. Louisa has drawings of the Taj I think. In the afternoon Marc drove me to see it. At the sound of its name I was very sick, for it has been the prime topic of conversation for so long; but notwithstanding this disadvantage I was not in the least disappointed. To attempt to give you any description of it would be utterly useless. You must be satisfied with knowing that I don't possess language that would enable me to give you the least idea of what I thought of its sublime beauty. I daresay you know the history of it; indeed, if you do not, it cannot be interesting to one who is never likely to see it. I may here mention that Lord W. Bentinck's name is never mentioned in this country but to execrate, and what now leads me to make the remark is that he actually proposed *selling* this most wonderfully magnificent edifice, and merely gave up the plan because he could not get the sum he wanted.* His system of economy was so great that he was ready to pull down and sell anything or everything, without reference to the harm it would do to the English rule in this country in the eyes of the natives.

The fort here is the most magnificent thing that mind can conceive. It was built by the great Akbar. Within the walls are also some of the most beautiful buildings

---

* This assertion was widely repeated and found its way into several reputable works, including William Sleeman's *Rambles and Recollections of an Indian Official* and E.B. Havell's *Indian Sculpture and Painting*. Careful examination of the evidence has led to the conclusion, however, that while Bentinck did order the sale of some marble at Agra – probably taken from a building too far ruined to be repaired – the story concerning his intention to sell the Taj is a *canard* born of his unpopularity in military circles. See Percival Spear, 'Bentinck and the Taj', *Journal of the Royal Asiatic Society*, 1949, pp.180–7.

imaginable, all of which we have visited. One is called the Pearl Mosque, and was built by Shah Jehan, the man whose ashes repose in the Taj. The next is called the private residence of Jehangir, who was the father of Shah Jehan. In the last building was pointed out to us a bare piece of wall which we were told had been the handsomest part of the whole of this most beautiful building, but Lord William had had it pulled to pieces and the inlaying marble etc. sold piecemeal for what it would fetch! About five miles from the city of Agra is the tomb of the great Akbar. This also I went to see, and Oh! it is so beautiful. It is altogether a most interesting city, and one ought to remain here for some time to have a clear and distinct impression left of its beauties. Our happiness was much interrupted in this way by the admixture of wordly concerns and by our having four successive dull dinners at Sir C. Metcalfe's. The poor well-meaning man also gave us a ball, and you may suppose what an affair it was when I tell you that there were but four unmarried ladies in the room, and their ages were fifty, thirty-three, thirty and eighteen. The eighteen-pounder was so ugly, vulgar, stupid, etc., etc., that she was in no request, and it was agreed that *I* was out and out the belle of the room. Ye Gods and all the Goddesses what think ye of this? I must conclude this now, for I want to despatch it from hence, and we leave the day after tomorrow. My father's boil is nearly well, and he is quite well. So are we all, and we send our love to yourself and all our friends and relations. So believe me, my dear Mrs Chaplin,

Very affectionately yours,

I. Fane.

Agra, January 3rd 1837. I wish you a very happy new year and many of them. We had *mince pies* and *plum pudding* on Christmas Day!

XII

We left Agra, my dear Mrs Chaplin, on Thursday the 5th of January. On our second day's march we reached a place called Futtehpore Sickri [Fatehpur Sikhri]. This place is famous for its ruins, as well as for a very sacred mausoleum, in which repose the ashes of a man named Selim [Sheik Salim Chisti]. The history of this man is as follows. The great Acbar [Akbar, Emperor of India 1555–1605] was likely to die childless, so in his distress he consulted this great man, whose advice he also took on other subjects. Selim desired him to send Mrs Acbar to him, and he would see what was to be done. In due course of time Mrs Acbar produced Jehangir [Jahangir, Emperor 1605–1627]. Acbar was most grateful, and not in the least suspicious, and when Selim died this beautiful tomb was raised over him out of gratitude. In the evening of our arrival we all rode to see all that was to be seen, and a most remarkable sight it was. We rode for a mile and a half I should think, up a road just wide enough to hold one horse, and behind and before and on each side was nothing but masses of ruin. It was the most extraordinary scene of devastation one ever beheld, and brought to one's mind the destruction of Pompeii, or Babylon, or some of those very wonderful overthrows of cities. Today, fortunately, happened to be the anniversary of the death of Selim, so when we arrived at the quadrangle in which his tomb is situated a most interesting and curious sight presented itself.

161

Thousands assemble here on this particular day, and a fair is held. In this country you cannot imagine how pretty a crowd is, for the colour in the dress of the natives is so various that it forms a beautiful *coup d'oeil*. We walked all through the fair and went into the tomb, which is inlaid with mother of pearl, and should have thought it beautiful had we not seen those at Agra.

We are coming a great bit out of our way for the purpose of seeing Bhurtpore [Bharatpur]. Today, January 9th, we reached it. By the bye, I have something to say about Saturday the 7th. Our camp was pitched close to what is here called a jungle, but what we English folk should call a wood, for it was exactly like the country about Apethorpe, and extends for many miles. I have been constantly lamenting since I began the march, never having seen any of the wild beasts of the country (as I call them.) This evening I rode out with Marc and Henry Fane into this jungle, and there I had my wishes amply gratified, for we saw two or three large herds of wild boars and pigs and pigglings. They were so impudent, and came so close and stared at us, that Marc did not feel easy in his mind at first, as we had no weapons of defence. However, they left us unmolested. Then we saw also large herds of antelope, jackals, foxes, peacocks and hares. The gentlemen had been out shooting in the morning, but had had very bad sport.

Now for Bhurtpore. We were to go three miles of our march in the carriage, that is my father and I and Christine. We were then to meet all the staff and a large portion of cavalry, and mount our elephants. A little further on the Rajah of Bhurtpore was to meet His Excellency. Oh, that I had the pen of a ready writer to describe this scene! The Rajah himself is not more than nineteen years of age, but is *so* fat and disgusting that he looks forty at least. He was beautifully drest in a gold kincob, and had a very pretty turban on his head, gold also, from which hung a large tassel of pearls. He had also very fine pearls in his ears. He was mounted on an elephant which had a very handsome howdah and trappings. He had an immense retinue, consisting of about thirty elephants, with camel riders, horsemen and foot soldiers, besides falconers with their falcons, who gave us sport as we went along, dogs to run after hares, cheetahs in case we fell in with antelope – in short the fun we had, as well as the dust, was quite indescribable. I wish you could have seen John. His face he now wears covered with whisker, which is of a very dark hue. The mass of dust which settled upon it, as well as upon his hair, eyebrows and eyelashes, so completely disfigured him that I do not think his nearest relation could have known him. I, being dark, was a tolerable figure also, but I tucked my hair away and so had only white eyebrows and lashes instead of my natural ones. The Rajah, with his retinue, accompanied us to the entrance to our camp and then took his leave for the present.

At twelve o'clock my father had a durbar, when the Rajah came in great state. At six he went to dine with him in the fort, with all his staff, general and personal. The Rajah wanted Christine and me to dine with him also. We were dying to do so, and thought we well might, for all the ladies of Governors-General and Commanders-in-Chief had fed with natives before us; but, notwithstanding these precedents, nothing would induce my father to let us. He got angry at my urging it, and wondered how we could wish to appear before a set of creatures who condemned us for the act. The Rajah was so civil, and said as we would not dine he would have a room prepared for us alone, where we might see the illuminations etc. This my father gave his consent to, so at seven o'clock Christine and I mounted our elephants, and accompanied by Major Byrne (a nice dear elderly man belonging to the staff, who has been in India all his life nearly and is perfectly conversant with

163

the habits and ways of the people, both high and low)
sallied forth for the Rajah's palace. We had about three
miles to go. It was a very pretty thing to see. The whole
of the exterior was a mass of light. We dismounted and
were conducted by the attendants to the room
appointed for us. There we found a table spread with
wine and tea in case we liked any. (N.B., I had some of
the latter, which was particularly nasty). After a little
we said we should like some nautch girls, who in the
style of Aladdin instantly appeared. We had three sets of
them, all beautifully drest, and two were very pretty.
We looked at them dancing and listened to their singing
until we were tired, and then got up to take our
departure, a message having been sent a few minutes
before to say my father was gone. The Rajah sent to
know whether he might come and salam to us, so we
said in return we would salam to him as we went out.
To our horror and amaze we were ushered into the
room where he was having a nautch, surrounded by his
court, squatted on the floor. We were requested to sit
down, which our advisers advised us to do for a minute
or so; so there we by accident found ourselves in the
very situation which my father disapproved. However,
we did not stay three minutes, and we mean that the
secret of our having been so entrapped shall *die* with us.

Tuesday 10th   My father, etc. went out shooting this
morning with the Bhurtpore Rajah. They had not good
sport, but my father seemed to have been altogether
pleased. The afternoon of this day Christine and I, Marc
and H. Fane went through the city on elephants. It is a
miserable place; the streets just wide enough to admit a
carriage, the residences mud, and all looking so dirty.
Dyeing seems to be the principal occupation of the
inhabitants. Their colouring matter is beautiful, but
they cannot dye fast colours. We also went into the fort,

which is of mud, and not interesting to any but military characters. The ditches around it are wide and deep. We also went and saw the spot the neglect of which on the part of the usurping rajah was the cause of the place's being so easily taken [by the British in 1826]. It was thus: there is a great lake hard bye, which by the opening of a sluice, fills the ditches with water. In his alarm the rajah forgot to attend to this, and the Company's troops instantly got possession of the spot. They took very good care not to let in the water, and this facilitated their manoeuvres very much. In our ride through the city and fortress we saw the Rajah's palace by daylight, and its grandeur was much diminished.

Wednesday 11th   After breakfast this morning my father went out shooting wild fowl with the Rajah of Bhurtpore. I am going to tell you something very ungenteel about him; but it is so funny a circumstance that I can't resist. The distinguishing mark in the dress of the Hindoo and Mussalman is that the one leaves his right bosom exposed to view, the other the left. This to you sounds shocking; but to us who are accustomed to see *both* at *once* all day long it is a trifle! But what I wish to observe is, that the Rajah's was an object never to be forgotten. I have told you how fat he is, and I do assure you that this machine of his hung down more than the biggest of ladies'. *I* should have been proud to have *half* as much, but *very* sorry to have possessed the whole! I beg pardon for my vulgarity!

Thursday 12th   This morning ended our halt and we left Bhurtpore at half-past six. The Rajah sent his cheetahs on with us to enable us to sport on the march. All sorts of plans had been adopted to enable me to see the fun also; but alas! in consequence of the stupidity of

165

M. Beresford's servants, and a little want of thought on his own part, they all proved abortive and I was compelled to bundle on to camp without falling in at all with the sportsmen. I was very much disappointed; but Marc was so unhappy I concealed my chagrin. At about four o'clock the whole of the city of Kumbahee [Kambahi] adjourned to our camp and filled up the street in hopes of getting a sight of His Excellency. When I went out of my tent to mount my horse there I found this immense crowd; and when I found for what they had assembled I went to my father. He said he would put on his red coat and walk across the street to gratify them, which he accordingly did, and they then dispersed. We encamped close to the fortress and city of the place I have named. It belongs to the Bhurtpore Rajah, and yielded without a blow when Bhurtpore fell. H. Fane, Dr Wood and I rode to see it in the evening. The city is of mud, dirty and ugly. There is a palace in the centre of it, which we went over; but it did not in the least reward me for the trouble of scrambling about it in my riding habit. The city is full of peacocks, which in the Bhurtpore district are highly venerated, and my father has issued an order that while we are marching through these territories none is to be shot on any account.⎯

Friday 13th   I tried my luck again this morning sporting, and in order to be in time I got up at half-past five o'clock and set off in my palanquin half an hour before the rest of the camp began to stir. It answered beautifully, for I arrived at the appointed spot about a quarter of an hour before my father and the rest of the sportsmen. The Persian Interpreter (a man whom we all like very much), Dr Wood and I took a line of our own. We had two cheetahs, three hawks and a lure buck antelope to ourselves. We fell in with immense herds of

166

animals and had two beautiful chases. The first the cheetah killed was a fine buck with beautiful horns, which I am to have. The second was a doe, and gave beautiful sport. I went for some distance on an elephant but when near the deer had to get on a machine drawn by bullocks, to understand which I refer you to a picture in the first volume of Captain Mundy's *Tour*, pages 48 & 51. I also saw very pretty sport with the hawks, who caught a hare and a partridge. The lure antelope did nothing. The wild ones would not find him; they were scared by the constant firing which was going on all around him and would not even approach him. I did not reach camp until half-past eleven, and then with a pain in my head from the sun, which had become very hot. We did not have the expected rain at Christmas, so the weather in the daytime is getting much hotter. The evenings, nights and mornings are still very cold. I forgot to tell you that three of four mornings ago my maid brought to my bedside a plate of ice about as thick as four wafers which had grown in the night on a jug outside my tent. This same day we reached a place called Deig [Dig], still in the Bhurtpore territories.

Saturday 14th   We reached a place called Goverdun [Govardhun]. It is the burial place of the ancestors of the present Bhurtpore Rajah. The place is in our possession, but the reigning man is most anxious to have it back, which I am not surprised at, for it contains some very beautiful tombs. But he won't get it, poor man, so he had better make up his mind to the loss. On Sunday afternoon I went to pass my judgement on them, and very much was I gratified with my visit. They are all of carved stone, very prettily worked on the exterior. The roof of the interior (dome-shaped) is painted in very vivid colours; but neither the subjects of these paintings nor the paintings themselves have any merit, further than the general effect. The swarms of monkeys here were quite incredible, and they were so tame and impudent. They as well as peacocks are held in this place highly sacred. It is altogether a most sacred place, and there are such quantities of faquirs. At one of the tombs sat one who had never stirred from his position for twelve years. Christine saw him; I did not, which I much regretted; but I did not even hear of him until it was too late.

Monday 16th   We had a long march to do this morning, and the road was so sandy and heavy that my bearers tumbled down with me in my palanquin; but no harm happened. We reached the city of Muttra [Mathura], which contains both civil and military. Our morning was agreeably occupied by receiving the visits of the ladies of the station. Five called. Fortunately they were all talkative and we did very well. One was well-drest and ladylike – Miss Reid by name – and she had received a Paris education. She was moreover pretty, although we had strong suspicion there was a vast deal of black blood in her veins. Three were ugly and vulgar and the fifth was said to be rather mad, but she showed no symptoms during her visit. In the afternoon my father inspected the stables, etc. of the cavalry which are quartered here, and Christine and I took the spare gentlemen and rode to see the city. After riding up some of its streets, which were as usual very narrow and dirty, we made for the river (Jumna), which we crossed by means of a bridge of boats. It looked well from the opposite side, for all along the banks are many very pretty ghauts, and in the centre of the city is a handsome mosque with very lofty minarets. In the course of our ride we fell in with a very distressing faquir (or religious mendicant), for he had not a rag of clothes on him, not so much as a *fig* leaf! And he was smeared from tip to toe with white dust, which gave him a horrid appearance. Muttra is a very sacred city, for here is said to have been born the Hindoo deity Krishna, and pilgrims come from far and near to pray and wash. You cannot fancy anything like the monkeys in this place; they are innumerable, and so impudent. About six miles from Muttra is a place called Kinderabund, where there is a ruin of an ancient Hindoo temple which we were told was worth seeing. Accordingly we took our carriage and four horses and set out to judge for ourselves. The road was so infamous and so dusty and the streets so narrow that actually to turn the corner of one we were compelled to get a lot of natives to lift us. Upon our arrival at the place we were by no means rewarded for our tedious journey. It was a very massive curious style of architecture, and would have been worth seeing at the end of three miles, but not so at the end of six. We bought here a rupee's worth of little brass gods (I should call them devils), which will look very curious and well on my table in my cottage in England when I am settled down as an old maid with my Persian cat by my side.

Saturday 21st   Today we reached a place called Allyghur [Aligarh] and here we experience the inexpressible felicity of being joined by our dreaded friends the Churchills. If they only knew the universal calamity it is considered, they would indeed feel flattered. Today we have heard a piece of intelligence which has grieved us much, but we hope it may turn out untrue. An account has been received of the death of Mr Deedes, whom I am quite sure Louisa must have heard of from our relations at Allahabad. Carry has been given in marriage to him by the gossips. The W. Fanes were very fond of him and I shall be truly sorry for his death. He died it is said on the banks of the

Nurbudda [Narbada], on his overland journey to England.

Sunday 22nd   I am truly grieved to say that today this melancholy report has been confirmed. He caught a fever at the place I have named and I suppose, poor young man, having no medical advice with him and being in bad health, he fell a victim of his malady. Here, as usual, we halted. I wish, dear Mrs Chaplin, you did but know what I have to go through every Sunday. I have told you Marc Beresford acts as clergyman when we are at a station where there is no church. Of course, he depends upon the congregation for responses, and the people are such *fools* they will not do it properly. There are three ladies in camp besides myself, whose services I have endeavoured to obtain by promising them *my* voice if they won't forsake *me*. One sits next to me during the service, and I give you my word that although our proximity is such, I can just hear her mumbling, and to my horror I often find my voice and perhaps *one* more the only voices audible, and yet I am obliged to go on, otherwise there would be no clerk at all. My heart beats, and my face gets so hot from these circumstances, which I know you can understand, for I know as well as possible yours would do the same. Devotion is out of the question, so great are my sufferings. Moreover today I have been told I showed my legs shockingly to two young men who sat behind me. If they were good, I should not care for this; but they are so *calfless*, so my troubles are great you see today!

    In the afternoon my father saw the troops, I am sorry to say; for although they went through no manoeuvres and the inspection was soon over, yet as he has been hitherto so properly observant of the Sabbath, I would rather (had I been consulted) there had not been a single exception. He could not very well help it, because we only arrived on Saturday, and he shot in the afternoon and we left on Monday morning. John drove me in the evening to see the fort. I believe it was strong when defended by General Perron (the Frenchman who aided the Mahrattas against our power, and whose services enabled them to hold up their heads a wee bit longer than they would have done without his aid); but it is not now kept up, and I assure you it required courage to pass the bridges over the ditches etc., for there was nothing on either side to prevent your going in if the horse shyed, and there were great holes in the road, through which you could see the water beneath. The roads here were so good, and such a very great treat after the sandy infamous things we had of late travelled over.

We have travelled on since Sunday as usual, but nothing occurred to relate until Tuesday night, when it rained cats and dogs and thundered and lightened and did everything that was disagreeable to people who live in tents; but it was much wanted and will be of great use to the country. For some little time the beauty of our appearance is spoilt. The tents, instead of looking white as snow, are a horrible mud colour, and upon our arrival yesterday morning we found the things which are spread on the ground by way of a carpet sopping, and everything in short damp and dirty.

Wednesday 25th   A horrible day. It rained tremendously, and was moreover so very cold. The 16th Lancers are marching to Meerut [Mirath] and here we joined their company. They swelled our camp to an immense size and were the cause of much amusement on the march of a morning – or rather their followers were. They make one feel quite odd, being surrounded again by so many white faces and hearing people speak in our own tongue. Today English letters reached us and I received your portion of journal bearing date

171

September 3rd to 15th. I was very nearly forgetting to tell you about that stupid fellow Edward Hodges. Fancy, after all the trouble by father took about him, and having succeeded in placing him in a situation which was likely to turn out very lucrative to him, he has allowed himself to be humbugged by Mr Harris, who has promised him 250 per annum more than he before gave him, and some horses, if he will return to his service. Without consulting or even communicating with my father until the deed was done, he has thrown over Mr Trotter and opium for his old business of indigo. I don't think he has acted altogether right, but he is so simple-minded he must be forgiven, and I only hope he will find that Mr Harris will keep to his word; but as he has before deceived him, he may again.

Friday 27th   This morning we reached a place called Haupper [Hapur]. One of the stud establishments for the supply of the Indian Army is situated here, so we halted for my father to inspect it, which he did in the afternoon.

Sunday 29th   We had prayers today as usual, in the durbar tent, which I just mention because I was today, and hope to be for the future, quite mentally comfortable. I made our new ladies, the Churchills (who are not in the least shy), promise to assist me in my office of clerk, which they faithfully did.

Tuesday 31st   This morning we reached Meerut. About five miles short of the station my father inspected the 11th Dragoons, who are leaving this place for Cawnpore. He has been much canvassed in the papers for this transfer, but whether justly or unjustly far be it from me to say. Meerut is a very nice station, therefore I

172

suppose those of the regiment who feel regret at leaving it abuse him for ordering them away. At 11 o'clock our fun began (that is, Christine's and mine). Ladies and their spouses inundated us from that hour until two. At last I got so exhausted I could scarcely find a word to say, I had run the sun, wind and dust so dry. In the evening I rode out with my father all round the cantonments, which are extensive and attractive. There is a plain, on which we are encamped, which extends for miles and miles, and if it was but green it would be beautiful; but in this country, excepting at one time of the year, everything is burnt-up and brown. The residences are also so nice here, and the gardens – both flower and vegetable.

Wednesday February 1st   The same fun in the visiting line took place, and the same exhaustion in me, only rather worse, for I have had an abcess forming in my ear for the last two days. This was so painful today that it rendered me somewhat unfit for exertion. Like a great idiot in spite of this I chose to ride out to see a tank about three miles from camp. The motion of the horse hurt me very much, as did the cold of the evening, and when I got home my ear was so bad that instead of going to a company dinner I put on a poultice and went to bed. I spent four wretched hours, and then I suppose the thing broke, for I went to sleep and got up much better. I was to have gone with one Mrs Hamilton (a sister of Captain Anson's, who came out in the *True Briton* with us) to a grand review this morning, Thursday 2nd, but after my sickness I thought it prudent to stay at home, the more so as I had a ball to attend in the evening. Mrs Hamilton is such a very nice, pretty, lady-like woman, by far the nicest we have seen in India. Her ball was particularly well attended, and we remarked the ladies were very, very well drest, and looking nicer than at any other station where we have yet been. We did not reach home until half-past one o'clock. I danced until my back ached terribly, and much ashamed I was of myself – or rather *am* of myself – for my folly in my old days.

Friday 3rd   This morning early there was a very beautiful artillery review; but on account of having been up late the night before and having had a surfeit of military spectacles I remained in bed. At ten o'clock there was an elegant breakfast given by the artillery at their mess room. This of course Christine and I attended. It was a very pretty sight, and very well attended, and for the hour or so I remained I was not much bored. But I got rather alarmed before we left, for it was buzzed about that dancing would be agreeable. Having only just left off I did not like the idea of beginning again, and as I am ashamed of my weakness at the more natural hour, I would have been much more so at this unnatural one. We escaped, though, unhurt.

I am going to give you a piece of intelligence which I think will please you, who are so staunch a supporter of Morrison and his Pills. Their fame has reached this country, and they are much patronized by several *scarecrows* we have fallen in with. But here is a man who would indeed delight your heart, for he boasts of having taken 2,800 himself, and not alone that, for he *feeds* his wife and child upon them; but – I am sorry to be obliged to add – although this sensible, discriminating character is a man of about sixty years of age you would take him to be ninety at least, and he has not a tooth in his head. Mrs Dennis, his wife, is quite a young woman, but looks like Mother *Bunch*, and trembles all over like an aspen leaf. Whether all this is the result of Morrison's thousands or not *you* will be better able to decide than I can. But I have my suspicions. The child at present is a fine specimen of a Benjamin.

174

My father was this evening entertained by a regiment here, called the Buffs. Marc Beresford and John belong to it. There was eating and drinking, and toasting went on; and the Colonel of it (the Morrison Pill man) paid my father sweet compliments. This man has a tongue which for length can vie with the chameleon's. He licks each nostril with ease when his pocket handkerchief is not handy. I forgot to mention that John and Captain Campbell went on Thursday night, after Mrs Hamilton's ball, on an expedition tiger shooting, thirty miles off. They are to be absent four or five days.

Saturday 4th   For my father military inspections in the morning early. Beastly visitors for us, which were very *mal à propos*. In the afternoon I was allowed to drive in the buggy with Marc. My father inspected stables, etc. and was entertained at night by the station. This seemed to be a low, nasty business, for lots got drunk early in the evening and made beasts of themselves. Christine and I, Dr Wood and Marc dined at home, but we were not pleasant on account of our tempers. We endeavoured to kill time with cards, and fortunately a drunken soldier got into our camp (a lancer) and settled himself down close to my tent. Marc was called to send him to the guard house, and so a diversion was made.

Sunday 5th   There is a very nice, pretty church here, to which we went at eleven o'clock. There are two clergymen also, both said to be Methodistical. One is at least obstreperous and ill-judged. He interferes in military matters and preaches from the pulpit at individuals, which I think so wrong. After church H. Fane drove me out in a buggy. I am tired of riding and driving at Meerut; it is so dull to go for a mile and a half

175

the same road night after night, and there is no other but what is very bad or very dusty. We had twenty to dinner, and we all did very well and talked well. Old Mrs Ramsay is a darling, for she made her old husband tell Andrew (who is their son) to call the carriage at a quarter before nine. General Ramsay is the brother of Lord Dalhousie.★

Monday 6th   Our visitors are diminishing rapidly. We had but one today, and she was very odd. I had her, Christine her husband. We were getting on swimmingly, as I thought, when all of a sudden, before I had scarcely finished a sentence, up she got and glided out. This funny proceeding was afterwards accounted for by our being told she was as deaf as a post, and had not heard a word I had said. This evening there was an immense dinner party of about eighty at General Ramsay's. I got placed next to an acquaintance, which was a great mercy. The dinner was most tedious, and very cold and nasty, excepting some curaçao, which was good and hot.

Tuesday 7th   Today my father gave us a piece of intelligence which has given him the greatest delight, and to Christine and I he has given the option of experiencing the same pleasure, as we like. It is as follows. The celebrated Runjeet Singh [Ranjit Singh – see Introduction] has written him an invite to Lahore, to visit him and to be present at the nuptials of his grandson, which will take place on or about the 19th of March. My father will be the first *great* man ever to have been at this great chieftain's capital; indeed the traveller Byrne★★

★ Commander-in-Chief 1829–31. Father of the famous Governor-General.

★★ Alexander Burnes, who was sent up the Indus with a gift of six dray horses for Ranjit Singh in 1831. The mission was a cover for a spying exercise, and it inaugurated the extension of British control over Sind.

176

is the only European who ever has. Lord W. Bentinck
had an interview with him, but he just crossed the
Sutledge [Sutlej] and was there met by R. Singh. He
went no further, so this is a great era in Indian history.
No doubt there is some political intention hid away
under this invite; but I am delighted that my father is the
man chosen for the purpose, for whatever it is I am sure
he will settle it well, and he is *so* pleased at the idea of
going. As you may suppose, I did not hesitate about
accompanying him. There seems to be a doubt whether
I shall be the only lady in camp who does go. They all
seem most anxious, but have pledges of affection who
stand in their way. The expedition may keep us out in
the plains longer than will be comfortable on account of
the heat, and this is supposed to be bad for these
darlings; therefore the parents and their encumbrances
will, from Kurnaul [Karnal] hurry on and ascend the
mountains in time for their darlings' health. I don't care
whether they go or not; but I shall be very sorry if
Christine's darling prevents her going. With this history
I shall conclude this portion of my journal. We go to a
station ball tonight, the third since we have been here. I
am so sick of them; tomorrow morning at half-past six
we leave this and we shall not be in bed until two. Our
route is changed entirely in consequence of our visit to
Lahore and we do not visit Delhi, which I regret, as I
want shawls. So with this adieu my dear Mrs Chaplin. I
send my love to all, and all send their love to you. Ever
believe me with sincere affection,

Yours

I. Fane.

177

XIII

Thursday February 9th   We left Meerut at half-past six this morning. It was hard work, for we did not leave the ballroom until one. It was a pleasant ball. I danced all night like an old fool. The supper was a very good one, and before we left it the gentleman who brought me in and whom I sat next to rose up and said: 'Gentlemen, fill your glasses. I have a toast to propose which I know you will all drink with the most heartfelt satisfaction'. The toast was 'Miss Fane and the ladies who had attended the ball'. I felt just as if I was going to faint. My father got up and returned thanks, and, thank God, the toasting here ended. Well, as I was saying we left the next morning and marched to a place called Sardhana. This used to be the place of residence of the Begum Sumroo.* She had built here, at her own cost, a very pretty Catholic church, for this was the faith she

---

* Widow of Walter Reinhardt, a German adventurer known as 'Somru' (*Sombre*) because of his swarthy complexion. Reinhardt had been granted the *jagir* (fief) of Sandhana in reward for military services to the Mughal Emperor, and after his death his widow had managed his estate and his private European-trained army with a mixture of ruthlessness, ability and cunning. Her assiduous cultivation of the friendship of the British was mainly responsible for her survival during both the anarchy that preceded their rise to power and the stability that followed it. Her Amazonian resilience and amorous appetite had attracted a certain folklore, which she cultivated further before her death (1836) by becoming a convert to Christianity. The legatee

178

adopted before she died. She had tried many! It was
built by an Italian who was in her service and is of a very
mixed style of architecture. The altar is very handsome,
of white marble inlaid with coloured stones in the style
of the Taj. She is buried there, and a monument is to be
sent out from England to be placed over her. We also
visited her residence. The exterior was rather handsome, but the interior was not worth looking at. There
was a very good portrait of her done by some English
artist. She was a portrait fancier, and round the principal
room hung a great many portraits of Europeans with
whom she was acquainted. The person to whom she has
left her wealth is on his way to England. Perhaps you
may see him. He is such an ugly, fat monster, as dark as
my shoe but dresses English. He is no relation to her,
but she called him her adopted son because he was the
produce of an adopted daughter. She never had chick or
child herself, although she had more than one husband.
She was a wicked but wise old woman. She had one of
her husbands got rid of somewhat in the style of Uriah
in the Bible.

Friday 10th　　We had more rain, and very heavy,
during the night of Thursday. This we bore with
patience and resignation; indeed, we were very grateful
for it, because it has made the weather again *perishing*,
and it is now so very desirable to have it cool, on
account of our change of route and our being, in
consequence of the fun we are to have in Runjeet's
dominions, out in the plains longer than is altogether

---

mentioned by Miss Fane was David Ochterlony Dyce, a great
grandson of Reinhardt. He went to England in 1838 and became a
social celebrity. He entered Parliament in 1840 and married the
daughter of Lord St. Vincent. He died in 1851, having been
declared insane.

desirable. Today we had to ford the Hindon river. Equestrians, elephant-riders and indeed pedestrians had no difficulty in crossing it, but the wheeled machines got into sad trouble – one of my father's in particular, which contained his dressing apparatus. This vehicle usually starts about seven o'clock and arrives at the new ground in the middle of the night. Upon this occasion, when we waded the river at past eight, there it was stuck tight. It had been there all night, and would have remained for ever had it been left to the natives. They have no sense, consequently no resource when in difficulty, and squat down and chatter, which is a bad method of getting out of a scrape. The troubles ended at last and everything arrived at the ground in due course. We halted today as usual and on Sunday afternoon Christine and I and two of our gents sallied forth on a picturesque excursion to see a pond, a banian tree and lots of monkeys, which were in the neighbourhood of our encamping ground.

Monday 13th Today we encamped near a native town which was famous for its manufacture in brass, sugar and *arrack*! Close to our encampment ran the Douab [Doab] canal, which runs from the foot of the hills to Delhi. This canal is merely for the purpose of *irr*igation and not for *nav*igation at all. It is very shallow, though of course in the rainy season it is much deeper.

Wednesday 15th This morning we ended our march by crossing the river Jumna. Our tents were pitched close on the opposite bank. We all crossed on elephants, and the water came up about to their stomachs. Few adventures occurred; indeed, I know of but one, and that was of a camel which fell down in the middle of the stream and threw its load (a tent). It turned out a wet and miserably cold day, and we could not do a thing out of doors. One of the gentlemen of the staff shot a huge alligator on the banks of the Jumna, which he had hauled into camp. I think they said it measured fifteen feet from the snout to the tail.

Thursday 16th   This morning we reached Kurnaul [Karnal], a large and healthy station. Quantities of military came out to meet my father. We ladies in the course of the morning received a certain portion of visitors, but we have not been so much bored as at other stations. Amongst the list was one General Allard, a French officer in the service of the great Runjeet. He is now on his return to his master after an absence of two years, and is the bearer of a letter from the French king. Upon this occasion he calls himself *ambassador*. He cannot speak a word of English; nothing but French and Hindostanee, so he put us all, save Christine, in a dreadful fright, because although many of us understood him perfectly, and no doubt could have talked to him also, yet our fears prevented us. Christine speaks like a Parisienne – and so she ought, as she received her education there. He is such a nice, gentlemanlike man, and wears a long, long beard, which is quite white and which he can twist round his ears. He also wears huge moustaches. His dress is peculiar and picturesque. He wears a blue cloth surtout military coat, much embroidered and confined round the waist by a broad gold band, which is fastened in front with a very large and handsome gold clasp. His trowsers are scarlet, and of a peculiar make at the bottom, inasmuch as they are made open and lace up with gold from the ancle to the knee. He had also an elegant waistcoat, which with a fine and immense diamond ring concludes my description. He is hurrying on before us to prepare for my father, and took his departure for Lahore in the afternoon.

At seven we dined with General Duncan, and the dinner lasted just two hours. We were three quarters of an hour after our arrival before we went in to the repast, then found it cold and horrid. I lost my heart to the old general, whom I sat next to. He was such a nice old man. When this occupation was over we had to attend a station ball and supper. I was much bored at the first and *very* much at the last – for there was toasting, which makes me so nervous. *My* health was drunk, and my father's, and I think he speaks very badly in answer; but I believe he feels shy before his family. We were not home until one, and we had to march the next morning at half past five. My father and staff remained to review the troops, and did not reach camp until eleven o'clock. It was such a *beastly* day, pouring with rain and so dreadfully cold. We had the stove all day, and sat round it wrapped up in shawls and boas, with cloaks round our legs, and yet could hardly keep warm. Would you believe this of India unless you had it from such undoubted authority! Today we caught sight for the first time of the Himalayas.

Saturday 18th   The rain had ceased today, to our great delight, for if it had not it would have been impossible to proceed. Our immense tents when saturated with rain are so heavy they are too much for the beasts of burthen; and the delay of a day now would be ruin to us, and prevent our reaching Lahore in time for the wedding. It was very distressing today to see the wretched camels. They tumbled about in such a manner. We saw many deposited in the bottom of ditches, into which they had slipped and were obliged to be dug out; however, none had *split* up, which is what usually happens when they travel after rain, and then they cannot stir again but are there left to be devoured by jackals, vultures, wolves or anything that likes. The gentlemen went out shooting today and had a little sport amongst the black partridge and hares. The former are reckoned great delicacies, but in all *our* opinions they are upon a par with all Indian game and are perfectly tasteless. In the evening my father and I, etc., rode to see a very holy tank in the neighbourhood. It must be very fine when full of water; but we found it quite empty, and the reason for its being so is that *we* have helped ourselves to the water for the use of the Douab canal. A funny scene took place here. There was a pundit who acted as cicerone, and who carried a book in which it appeared to be the custom for English travellers to write down their names and nonsense. He was most anxious to be possessed of my father's autograph, and so was another man who was possessed of a book also. My father put out his hand to satisfy the first petitioner, and such a scramble took place between the two. This sort of proceeding in England would be reckoned quite innocent and natural; but for a black man to act so towards a white is reckoned by old Indians the height of impertinence; and I thought Captain Hay (the Persian Interpreter), who is a very mild man, would have murdered them. I am quite sure that had Captain Campbell been of the party he would have done so outright, for he holds the nation in such sovereign contempt. The result was that the first gained his point. The over-anxious man did not. We also rode through the city [Thanasar], which would have been rather nice, only there was a dirty drain ran right down the centre of it, which produced a villanous smell.

Ever since we left Kurnaul we have been in the territories of the Seiks [Sikhs]. They are independent, but *protected* by us; and upon the occasion of sueing for this our countenance, when they were once in trouble by quarrelling amongst themselves, we *kindly* gave it them upon condition they gave us Loodiana [Ludhiana]. So they did, and here we have a nice healthy station in

183

the midst of their dominions. They are a fine hand-some race of men, very fair, with a great deal of very black beard. Several of their chiefs have visited my father. They all envelope themselves in beautiful shawls, which I much covet, and all present my father with matchlocks. He is so detestably conscientious that he returns them all, though now that he is in independent states he might keep them.

Sunday 19th   We could not afford time to halt today. We have daily now beautiful views of the mountains and snowy range. Whilst we are in the Seik dominions we may not kill any beef, they reverence anything of the cow kind so much. They will not kill to *eat* one, but they don't scruple to ill-treat one to death.

Monday 20th   We reached Umballa [Ambala] this morning; a great place for the manufacture of shawls. We sent for some to look at; and although they were not the best sort, there was one I should have liked – but it was beyond my means.

Tuesday 21st   My father had a fall from his horse this morning. He was riding a new one that he has just got from the stud, and it frisked and turned short round. He would not have tumbled off from this, but it struck him in the face with its head, and knocked him off. He was not a bit hurt to signify and the only result is a bloodshot eye, which gives him no inconvenience. This evening Christine and I, John and H. Fane went to see a serai, or caravanserai, which was near our camp. These are no longer used as they were originally intended to be, but are turned into villages, and travellers who might like to spend the night therein are obliged to do so outside.

Wednesday 22nd   We had a very long march to do today to a place called Sirhind. In the afternoon my father had to dress quickly to receive a visit from a great native known by the name of the Puttialah [Patiala] Rajah. He came in immense state, mounted on a beautifully caparisoned elephant and seated in a very grand-looking, but wretchedly uncomfortable howdah. We ladies have established a lovely peeping place for these occasions, where we can see all that is going on without being seen. Unfortunately on this occasion it was so late when the man arrived, and so dark, we could see but little in the tent. The Rajah is a very fine man, taller than my father and as far as I could judge looked handsomely bundled up in shawls and finery of all kinds. His visit was short. I don't know whether you are aware that when the visit*ed* has had enough of the visit*or* attar is sent for and the pocket handkerchiefs of the greatest people present sprinkled with it. This is a hint for the people to depart, which they invariably take.

Thursday 23rd   There are very extensive ruins in the neighbourhood of our camping ground today (I ought to have mentioned we stole a halt to refresh both man and beast), so Christine and I, attended by five gents, went forth to see them. Sirhind is the name of the place. It was during the time of the Delhi kings an immense city, but it was then sacked by the Seiks, and every soul, man, woman and child, massacred. The ruins extend for miles in every direction, and although very curious they are not nearly so striking as those of Futtehpore Sickri, which I mentioned to you in a prior journal.

Friday 24th   About an hour before we commenced our march this morning it began to rain torrents; but as time is so precious we could not allow of its making any difference, so we all set off in our respective ways, I in my palanquin. The rain continued incessantly and after about three miles it became so slippery that my bearers could hardly get on and my patience was exhausted. The folks on the road were very amiable and offered me all sorts of conveyances, for all my own were far in advance. At last I got into a buggy belonging to Captain Hay, and Marc drove me into camp, which I reached dry and safe.

Saturday 25th   We encamped today near another serai, which must have been very handsome formerly. There were over some of the gateways remains of fine enamelling. I rode round and through it in the afternoon, and fell in with a wedding party who were on their way to a place we had just left to pick up the bride. The bridgroom was a boy of about fourteen. Christine's maid and mine had fine fun, for they were so civil to them and invited them to their tents. They remained outside and saw some nautching. Christine's was in raptures, and so was baby, for neither had seen anything of the kind before. The former liked it for itself; the latter on account of the glittering dress of the nautch girls.

Sunday 26th   We marched today to Loodiana, one of the great places for shawls. Some were brought for me to look at. They looked very handsome at a distance, but were very coarse when seen near, and even these far exceeded my means! My father inspected the troops stationed here in the afternoon. I joined him afterwards and accompanied him to the fort, which is great but strong enough only to keep off predatory Seiks. At this

186

station reside the ex-King of Kabul* and his family. One of them is the man from whom Runjeet Singh took the immense diamond** he has in his possession. He treated him barbarously until he obtained it.

Monday 27th   Upon our march this morning a vakeel [*vakil* – envoy] belonging to Runjeet came out with his troops, about forty in number, to meet my father. They drew up in a line and saluted him as we do and played *God Save the King*! It was not so well executed as our bands could do it, but it was very astonishing to hear it and *know* it in the heart of the Seik states. At Loodiana our escort was immensely increased and now consists of one squadron of H.M. 16th Lancers, two companies and band of H.M. 13th Light Infantry, two flank companies of the 2nd Native Infantry, one troop of Horse Artillery, and a wing of the 18th Native Infantry, under Captain Anson. I am afraid you will not understand the merits of all this. If you do, you are much more clever than I am, for *I* don't, although I am on the spot. I only know that our camp is immense, and that it is all to cut a splash for our great entertainer. We fire our own big gun now morning and evening and are altogether truly military.

Thursday March 2nd   On the march this morning one of my palanquin bearers was *took* with so bad a King

---

* The luckless Shah Shuja-ul-Mulk, who had been expelled from Afghanistan in 1809 and whom the British were to attempt to reinstate as a puppet of their own in 1839. He represented the Sadozai clan of the Durani tribe. During his exile the old Durani kingdom of Afghanistan was divided between three members of the Barakzai clan, of whom the most important was Dost Muhammad of Kabul.

** The famous *Koh-i-Nur* ('Mountain of Light'). It was confiscated from the Sikhs by the British after the second Sikh war (1849) and presented to Queen Victoria. Now in the British Crown Jewels.

Agrippa [*grippe* – influenza] he could not come on, and I was in great danger of being left on the road, or at least of arriving very late in camp, when Marc, who is ill from a knock he gave himself in the side, came past in his buggy. Although I am forbidden for the sake of appearance to be driven *much* by him, I thought this calamity sufficient excuse, so in I stepped, and glad I was to do so, for I look upon palanquin travelling as a dead loss in a new country and am very fond of a buggy. We encamped today about four miles from the Sutledge; so in the evening Christine and I and some of the gentlemen rode out intending and hoping to see some fun in the shape of accidents happening to the people and baggage who had to cross; but we found we had not time to go so far. We had people to dinner and would have been late.

Friday 3rd   This morning we crossed the Sutledge ourselves. There was a large covered boat to take over my father and his male and female staff, and quantities of others for taking over the troops, camels, elephants and all the innumerable etceteras of our present enormous camp. One of the poor sensible elephants fancied the boat in which he was put was not strong enough for his weight, so without making the least fuss he quietly stepped over the side and swam ashore. On the opposite side of the river were encamped Runjeet's son and troops, who had been sent down to meet and escort my father for the rest of the march through his father's dominions. You cannot imagine a prettier sight than the junction between the two powers. For a few hundred yards the ground formed a platform, upon which were assembled Shere Sing [Sher Singh]★ and his men and

★ Putative son of Ranjit Singh. Succeeded to the throne of Lahore after the death of Ranjit's acknowledged heir, Kharak Singh, in 1840, and was assassinated in September 1843.

His Excellency and his cavalcade. The banks then rose precipitously. I cannot describe to you how very pretty it was to see the procession losing itself through the fissures in the high banks. I bustled on, and reached camp a few minutes before my father. I was by this means enabled to see what took place. My father and his attendants, with Shere Sing and his, drew up side by side in front of our tents, whilst the whole of our escort troops marched by (the band playing), which they did to the satisfaction of the Commander-in-Chief. This done they all dispersed, and we all quietly dressed and went to breakfast. At four o'clock my father held a durbar, and Shere Sing visited him in great state. Christine and I retired to our peeping place, where we saw all that went on as plainly as if we had been in the room. He is a fine-looking man, with a pleasing countenance and white teeth, for the Seiks don't eat that horrible mixture which ruins and renders so very disgusting the mouths of the Hindoos. He was very handsomely drest in Benares kincob, and had very fine jewels in his headgear. The Seik dress is exceedingly graceful, and not military-looking. The colours they wear are very gay. Their trowsers, which are rather tight to their legs, are perhaps green or amber-coloured satin. Their coat, which is tunic-shaped, is of amber satin also; and over their shoulders they put on most gracefully a long wide silk scarf with gold borders and ends, some wearing white and some a brilliant scarlet. This mixture of colours perhaps does not read well, but you cannot think how gay and well it *looks*. Shere Sing travels on an elephant, seated in a silver howdah. This is the man who, if there be war at all upon Runjeet's death, will be the instigator of it.

As soon as Shere had left the durbar tent, one of his attendants brought in to present to my father a huge bag of rupees. I need not tell you what became of that, for you know how presents of all kinds are disposed of. Whilst we are in his dominions we are not to *purchase* a thing, but he is to furnish at his own expense all the provisions for the whole of our camp. Upon a rough guess it is supposed we now consist of 20,000 souls, and it is calculated we shall cost him a lack [lakh] of rupees, i.e. £10,000. His liberality commenced yesterday and the result was that both man and beast were starved; but this was accidental, the new system not having begun to act properly! We had Captain Wade, the Political Agent, to dinner, and a very great booby he seems to be.

Saturday 4th   In consequence of there having been on a previous occasion, *viz* when Sir C. Metcalfe once passed through these states, a fight between some of our people and the Seiks, my father has issued very strict orders that nothing is to leave camp after a certain hour at night, and that in the morning nothing of any sort or kind is to precede him. This morning was the first march after this order. I had no means of conveyance but my palanquin, and as I could not start before His Excellency I wish you could but see the trouble I got into. Carts, bullocks, artillery horses, led horses, sick beds, besides thousands of other things which if I were to mention you would not understand, were bumping and knocking me about on all sides. At last it became so disagreeable and dangerous I could not bear it and resolved to mount the first elephant I met with. Just as I had made up my mind to this I fell in with the baby and its maid, whose bearers had been knocked down. They were turning out and mounting Henry's elephant, and I went with them. We then got on famously, and I fell well on my legs, for I afterwards got a lift of ten miles in Mrs Torrens's carriage. In consequence of our having entertained the night before and the food plates, dishes and all the eating and drinking apparatus not being able to go on until a late hour, we got into a pretty scrape. The strict orders issued by my father told against himself, for the authorities would not allow his

190

very own things to proceed that night at all; so upon our arrival in camp after a march of eighteen miles we had not a morsel to eat or drink nor a prospect of getting a bit for hours. However, some of the staff were more fortunate, and they took compassion on us. Our own people got breakfast some at one place, some at another. My father and I had some tea and biscuits sent us by the Quarter-Master General. I did not mind it at all, for this is the first thing the least bordering on a hardship we have had to undergo, and it was but a trifle, after all.

In the afternoon my father and staff went to return Shere Sing's visit. Some of the aides-de-camp, amongst them H. Fane, or Edward as we sometimes call him, went by invitation into Shere's private apartments. They found he slept on a kind of bed, here called a charpoy, which is a low thing standing on four low legs shaped just like large balls. These were of silver. It has nothing by way of a canopy. He had a nice dressing table with drawers *à l'Anglaise*, upon which stood a looking glass and several *French* bottles with scent – that is to say, sandalwood and attar of roses. The parties were mutually pleased with each other.

Sunday 5th   This morning I again travelled on an ele-phant with Christine half the march, the other half in the carriage with Mrs Torrens. We had to pass close to a village in which reside a set of priesthood known by the name of Ackalees [*Akalis*]. They are a very lawless race. Even the great Runjeet himself has little or no authority over them, although they are in fact his best soldiers. This must proceed from their creed, for they think them-selves immortal, and therefore death has no sting to them. We did not see one of them on this occasion, although we were to have been insulted by them. After I got into the carriage with Mrs Torrens I had a most agreeable and amusing drive. The Seik people rode alongside of us, and as Mrs Torrens can speak their language pretty well, we had much conversation with them. They were perfectly respectful and well-behaved, and assured us it was their earnest desire to please us. They remarked that we wore no ornaments, and said *their* women wore a great many; upon which Mrs Torrens replied it was our custom to wear ours of an evening, and that *we* had a *great* many also! In the afternoon I rode with my father round our immense camp. He wanted to look how the troop horses appeared after their long marches. Edward and I continued our ride and fell in with a Seik on horseback, who seemed astonished at me and as if he wondered much where my *legs* could be. He spoke to us, but unfortunately we could not understand him, which I much regretted.

Monday 6th   Soon after we left camp, my father was met by another of Runjeet's sons, Khurrack Singh [Kharak Singh]. He came on an elephant, attended by an immense retinue, but dismounted and rode when he joined my father. This addition to Shere's cavalcade and my father's own formed a most beautiful *coup d'oeil*. All the lady camp followers this morning marched on elephants. We joined company and had a Seik guard to protect us, with a confidental man of Runjeet's to command them. They took great care of us. We managed so well we had a capital view of the procession, although we could not distinguish individuals. Upon our arrival at camp, three miles beyond Umritsar [Amritsar], we found pitched close behind my father's a beautiful little shawl tent, with a lovely shawl bed therein, which was a present from R. to H.E. – one of those pleasant presents, made to look at and long for! Also a charpoy bed, with lovely shawl mattresses, pillows and coverlids, one for each of the staff. Looked at in the same way.

The Gustavus of India we found today had pitched his camp about two miles from ours, so at eleven o'clock about, my father was to go and have his first interview with this great man. Runjeet sent his elephants for him, and the one on which my father got was beautifully caparisoned. The howdah looked like a lovely French china plate, being composed of a rich blue and gold material that looked like enamel. He was in full military costume, and wore all his orders, with the collar of the G.C.B. He was attended by all his staff, and a great retinue of soldiers. What I am now going to tell you, alas, alas! is only what I have collected from hearsay and questioning, for in this nasty country, as I have before told you, it is incorrect for females to take part or lot in a show. Runjeet came half way to meet my father, and when they met my father got into the same howdah with him. The cannons did indeed then roar for some minutes. They then proceeded to the durbar tent; and for Runjeet to dismount without spoiling his shoes, a lovely-drest man went down on all fours, and he stepped on his back. The interior of the tent was magnificent, but small, and composed of shawls. He is too much of a military character to dress effeminately, so his costume was simple, and consisted of green cashmere, without ornament, except some handsome pearls and diamonds. Of course, on gala days he has the *means* of being very magnificent; but I suppose as he was receiving a *warrior* he wished to appear one also. Some of his courtiers were superb, and there was a most tempting display of jewellery. His appearance pleased my father much more than he had been led to expect from the prints he had seen of him. He is a little man, and has lost one eye from the ravages of smallpox; but the other is a piercer and, John told me, like Lord Westmorland's, so it must be *pretty*, at all events! His face is much disfigured with the same malady, and he has an immensely long beard. He has lately had a paralytic seizure, which has affected his speech; and, being aware of this, he is much more silent than he used to be. But his mind remains the same, and a great one it is. At this visit compliments only were the order of the day, and presents were presented. My father received horses, elephants, beauteous shawls, jewellery and lots of money; was daubed with attar; and departed.

At three o'clock they all again went forth, attended by Runjeet and bound to the city of Umritsar for the purpose of visiting the bridegroom in honour of whose nuptials my father was invited into these dominions. I don't think I ever told you about this bridegroom, who he is, etc. Runjeet has three sons, *viz* Khurrack, the eldest and favourite and heir apparent; Shere and Tarra [Tara]. Shere and Tarra are twin brothers, and are by a different mother from Khurrack's. Runjeet doubts their being legitimately his. It is a great pity, for Khurrack is a booby and lout, whilst Shere is a fine fellow. The army is with Shere, so probably when Runjeet departs Khurrack will be in a bad way. The youth who is about to be married is Khurrack's son, and a great favourite with his grand-papa. At three o'clock on the day of which I am now writing, my father was to go, much attended by his own people and accompanied by Runjeet and his, to visit this bridegroom at his house in Umritsir. A bag of rupees, supplied for the purpose by the Political Agent, was thrown by my father from his howdah amongst the populace. This, I am told by eyewitnesses, produced a very amusing scramble. Nothing very entertaining took place at the residence of the bridegroom. It was the day on which all the money which the different landholders etc., etc. are obliged to give upon an occasion of this sort was collected. The young man also had a veil put on him, which is the custom in this odd country, and a very odd veil it seemed to be, composed, as far as I can understand, of strings of pearls and other stones tied on his forehead and hung down over his face. There were plenty of nautch girls, and the good-for-nothing men, both married and single, young and old, came home in an ecstasy at their beauty. Henry says they were no darker in their complexions than I am, and had beautiful features and such beautiful teeth.

The parties did not return until seven o'clock, and then we all had to go and dine with Captain Wade, the Political Agent, in his tent. We were all cross about it, because we disliked it so much. We had to go over ditches and banks and fields of corn for a mile and a half, and then our reward at the end was the nastiest and worst dinner I ever saw. Scarcely anything to eat, and the little there was the essence of garlic. Amongst the guests were the three French officers who are in Runjeet's service. General Allard, whom I have before mentioned, sat next to me, which as you may suppose gave me *infinite* delight; however, I thought no one would hear my bad French and therefore determined to do my best. I was astonished at myself, I got on so well and talked so much. No doubt it was fine stuff. It rained cats and dogs whilst we were at dinner, and thundered and lightened very much. We had fireworks furnished by Runjeet and had exhibited the presents which were offered in the morning, consisting of shawls, silks, muslins, kincobs and jewellery. But the former were not very good, and native jewellery, generally speaking, is so ugly.

Tuesday 7th   In order to avoid the crowd and confusion which is now to be met with along the road, I did not leave camp until an hour after my father, and had two Seik soldiers and one black dragoon to take care of me. I got on famously *per* carriage. I fell in with some of Runjeet's artillery, and was able to draw a comparison between ours and his; and although his are very wonderfully mounted and appointed, I could not but think that neither he nor his successors had better war against us! We were kept waiting a long time for our breakfast, and for this reason – Runjeet won't allow us to purchase anything. He intends we should be supplied gratis. This is so badly managed we cannot get anything without the greatest difficulty, not even wood to light a cooking fire. We had none this morning for some time after our arrival. One of Runjeet's officers informed his master of the distress we were in for wood, and his reply was truly characteristic of a despot: 'Why did you not pull down the village rather than let the General want?'! It rained and thundered etc., etc. very much this afternoon; but, notwithstanding, at seven o'clock Captain Hay and John were sent to Runjeet's tent with a complimentary message. They were instantly invited in and found the great man seated in a small tent, on the ground, surrounded by his favourites. He was eating his dinner, which consisted of quail curry, and they all helped themselves out of the pot, which was on the fire. Our two gents partook of the feast. This was washed down with drink so potent that half a wineglass-full would have intoxicated one of our people; but R. drank it like water. He was very pleasant and facetious, asked lots of questions both political and commonplace, and would have detained the parties much longer had it not been that Captain Hay, in order to get away, said that he should incur His Excellency's highest displeasure did he not quickly let him know of His Highness's health! Soon after their return R. sent my father a present of nine funny-shaped bottles of his favourite beverage. We all took a taste and I do assure you it was like liquid fire. Although we only put our lips to it our throats were burnt. No wonder the poor man has a broken constitution and paralytic tongue when this is his mode of living. A European doctor has been attending him, and has Galvanized him. They say he might get

196

quite well, but he will not submit to the necessary discipline.*

Wednesday 8th   Today great things went on, connected with the wedding. Quantities of money were to be thrown amongst the assembled multitude and my father was to assist in the distribution. At three o'clock about, and before we had quite finished our dinner, two of the French officers who are in the Maharaja's service came to say a deputation was waiting to conduct my father to the place where he was to join Runjeet. Everyone instantly mounted their elephants; and my father having given us leave to sally forth and see what we could without getting in the way, we sent the pleasing intelligence to the other ladies in camp, who joined us company, and off we set with a Seik mounted guard to ourselves. The scene was a most extraordinary one. Picture to yourself *thousands* of the very handsome Seik men, mounted on their handsomely caparisoned horses and drest in their very gay and picturesque costume of scarlet and yellow; quantities of elephants with magnificent howdahs, quantities with a plainer kind, quantities with only pads – in short, go on picturing and still you will fall *far* short of the reality of this most curious and interesting spectacle. We managed beautifully, and saw nothing to annoy us but everything to please us. Several wretched creatures were knocked down and crushed to death, but I believe upon the whole not so many as one might have expected in so dense a crowd. At length the procession reached the house of the bride's father, where the bride also was, and the bridegroom was then and there delivered up and

* His heavy drinking on this occasion (which he reckoned due to the demands of hospitality) further undermined Ranjit Singh's health and hastened a second paralytic stroke. This occurred in the winter of 1838, and was followed by his death in June 1839.

all the religious part of the ceremony was performed. The bride is ten years old. Everyone dismounted and my father was introduced to the bride's father. There was nautching, but this part of the business does not seem to have been entertaining. *They* of course did not see the lady, nor did *we* go into the house, which by the way was a large scrambling building, but very *ramshackle*. Having seen many of our friends dismount, we bent our steps homewards and reached camp safe and sound and much gratified with all we had seen. My father had a most fortunate escape from being *killed*; but he escaped, thank God, unhurt. His elephant moved as he was dismounting, but he clung to the howdah until he regained his footing. If he had fallen he would have dropped eighteen feet, they tell me, and *must* have been crushed by the animal. They returned home to tea by about seven o'clock, and immediately after we all, Christine and I also, again set out to see the grand display of fireworks exhibited at the Maharajah's tent in honour of the day.

Thursday 9th   This morning we had but three miles to march, so I waited until the confusion had subsided and then got into my palanquin, and Marc (who is ill with a pain in his back) and I groaned along together. No wood to light a fire for breakfast could be procured for some time. At three o'clock my father went, accompanied by his great entertainer, to see more money distributed to the needy, as well as to see more presents presented for the use of the *nouveaux mariés*. These consisted of shawls, jewellery, silver washing utensils, horses, buffaloes, elephants, camels, etc., etc.; 101 of each of the four-legged animals. This Christine and I did not go to because we were told it would not be worth seeing; but on their return they reported it was, so we have determined to skip nothing else. There were more fireworks this evening, and they were very fine; far superior to those of the evening before. The Maharajah had a great nautch in his pavilion, but my father did not attend it, which I was glad of, for I am afraid of his being too condescending. Christine and I and Captain Campbell took up our position of the night before, were equally politely treated, saw lots of beautifully drest nautch girls and magnificently drest men (the whole scene was so like a scene in a play); and having looked enough went home. There was a slight shock of an earthquake about ten o'clock tonight, but I was asleep and it was not enough to wake me. Several in camp felt it. Slight shocks are common occurrences in the Punjaub.

Friday 10th   We marched eleven miles today, and although I did not start until an hour after everyone else I got into a *mêlée* with the troops notwithstanding, and there was an old bluff commanding officer who was very cross to me and would not assist me to get through them. I had other friends at court, however, who helped me in my trouble, and I at length got past them. We had no festivities today, but in the afternoon Captain Hay and Henry (my brother) were sent to civilize to Runjeet. They had a pleasant visit, and the poor old man was so anxious to know how he could manage to give a remembrance to all in camp and ensure its not being taken by government. He was told, of course, it was impossible, quite. He is very anxious to consult our medical man, and another who happens to be travelling with us as an amateur, about his paralytic tongue. No doubt consent will be given, with a caution, but all will be useless unless he chooses, good man, to alter his mode of living. My father sent him a present of some brandy (very weak stuff to his palate), sherry and port wine from his own cellar.

Saturday 11th We only journeyed four miles today, and this for the purpose of being near a residence and garden of the Maharajah's called Shalemar. They are mentioned in *Lalla Rookh* [by Tom Moore]. He is going to give an entertainment there, but we females are not to see him, and fancy the misery of our not having yet been permitted to do so. I am downright cross about it. Modesty is a pretty thing, but I think in a case like this one might be allowed to overstep the mark by the breadth of a hair so as to be enabled to see so great a curiosity as he is.

Sunday 12th I was driven to despair this morning from the disappointment I experienced at being told we were not to see the Maharajah today, having been promised the night before that we would be introduced to him at a party he was to give. I dreamt of him all night in consequence! However I was consoled in the course of the day by receiving from my father's own lips that we should all be presented at Lahore in proper form. There is an Englishman of the name of Vigne* in our camp just now, who has been a great traveller in Cabul and Cashmere. He is an excellent draughtsman, and has made some beautiful sketches with a view of sending them to England, that a panoramic exhibition may be made from them. So if you should hear of a panorama from drawings by Mr Vigne about to be exhibited before we return to England, you must be one to patronize it. He brought them today, at my request, to show me, and I was much delighted with his portfolio altogether; but what gave me the greatest satisfaction was his kindly promising to do me a likeness

---

* Godfrey Vigne. Author of *A Personal Narrative of a Visit to Ghuzni, Kabul and Afghanistan* (1841) and *Travels in Kashmir, Ladak, Iskardo etc.* (1842).

of Runjeet. He has by stealth done one or two sketches pronounced to be exceedingly like. The old boy will not let him set regularly to work, from pure vanity. If he had *two* eyes they say he would like to have his picture taken. The prints of him are not in the least like, and that one which is the frontispiece to Prinsep's work, and which I think I have seen at Fulbeck, is particularly *un*like. At six o'clock this evening all the ladies in camp joined company and set off in palanquins for the Shalemar gardens, where Runjeet was to give my father an entertainment. A place was prepared on the top of the house for us *unfortunate* females, from whence we were to see the illuminated gardens, fireworks and all the fun. A beautiful little tent was here pitched also for our accommodation. The exterior was composed of crimson velvet, richly embroidered in gold; the interior was lined with shawls. The *coup d'oeil* from this was exceedingly beautiful, and the only manner in which I can at all give you an idea of the scene is by saying that it was a small Vauxhall; but at the same time I must candidly confess I think our Vauxhall gardens are far superior to those of Shalemar, both with respect to their laying-out as well as to their brilliance on a gala night. We sent for nautch girls, and amongst the lot we had the beauty our gentlemen so much admired on a previous occasion. She was very fair, and had a very handsome face, but a horrid figure; and she looked so very naughty. A number of the natives now intruded on our intended seclusion, and there were also a number of English officers present. The scene became more disorderly than we liked, so we only looked at these nasty naughty creatures for a very few minutes, pushed through the crowd and regained our palanquins. I was again nearly killed by a frightened elephant, which was within an ace of upsetting my palanquin, but I was not aware of my danger at the time. My father must have been considerably bored, for he had nothing to do but *jaw*, drink that terrible stuff of Runjeet's, look at fireworks – which is not in his line – and eat quail-curry.

Monday 13th   We marched about four miles this morning and encamped a short distance from the city of Lahore. Some people talk of the face of the country about here as having improved, but I think their imaginations very lively who say so, for to me it is the same dead flat. But the cultivation about is much and rich. You have no idea of the little regard these people have for their neighbours' property. They as readily take their baggage carts, etc. through a beautiful cornfield as they would through a ploughed field, and the destruction that has taken place since we began our march through the Seik territories must be immense; but it is said Runjeet intends to excuse these cultivators a year's rent. The other morning I saw about twenty pieces of Runjeet's artillery dragged through a beautiful crop, although the road was close by; and our camp is at this moment pitched in the midst of cultivation.

Tuesday 14th   We passed a very fatiguing morning actually doing nothing but looking on at the preparations which were taking place to get the tents right for a grand durbar, Runjeet being about to visit my father. As usual, we arranged a peeping place, and all the ladies in camp were invited to come and take their chance with us of getting a sight of the great man. At four o'clock all the troops were out and lined the street on either side, and the band was in attendance. Many of Runjeet's troops also assisted in keeping order. At that hour my father and suite mounted their elephants and went half way to meet our Buonaparte, as is the custom of the country. From our peeping place we had an excellent view of him as he was led up to his chair by my father.

You will like to hear he had his own chair, which is silvery-looking. Upon this he sits down, and then tucks up his legs under him in true oriental style. He appeared feeble, and his figure rather bent; but he was in excellent humour, seemed very happy and asked quantities of questions. He brought with him his son Shere, his prime minister and the prime minister's brother, a very handsome man who goes by the name in camp of Malek Adel. This man's dress is magnificent, and he has quantities of pearls about him. At this durbar he retired from the room into a corner close to where we were concealed and from whence we looked down upon him. We were curious to know the result of this manoeuvre, and what do you think in private this mass of splendour was guilty of? Would you believe it, he actually blew his nose in his fingers.

Today presents were made to him and his on the part of Government. We saw them laid out, and a vast deal of trumpery there was. There were horses presented, and two very good ones. One was a horse of H. Fane's, by which he has made money, I am happy to tell you, and Captain Campbell the same. Marc also got rid of an ugly (though he did not think it so) but good horse at prime cost. He received some excellent guns, pistols and swords, particularly one of the latter, the blade alone of which was valued at £400, the tempering was so beautiful. Then there was jewellery (native), which with a few exceptions I don't admire, and pieces of kincob and satins and silks and muslin, and one or two ugly and coarse coloured Europe muslins. After sitting for a long time talking, he went into the other tent to look at these, and then he took his departure. We were not sorry when he did, for the heat was very great in our small quarters; and here I may observe that our midday cool weather is gone. The mornings and evenings are very nice, but we shall be well stewed no doubt before we reach the hills. A dinner party ended our day's fun.

Wednesday 15th   I felt so miserable all the morning, because General Allard had promised to come himself and bring another of the Frenchmen to pay us a morning visit. They did come, and lunched with us, and very much bored I was. Mr Holroyd arrived today. Fancy his being such a *game* man as to come all the way from Calcutta expressly to take part in what is going on here. He has, after many adventures on the road, arrived in excellent time, for we have yet a week's amusement before us and something to do and see every day. This afternoon Runjeet exhibited to my father all his irregular troops. Christine and I intended to have gone, but unfortunately we did not think sufficiently for ourselves, and all our guard was taken from us. Without one it is impossible to stir here, so we were compelled to stay at home, and wretched and cross we were about it. It was represented to be a most curious sight. Amongst them were 500 of those fanatics whom I have before mentioned, called Ackalees, who make a most savage display. They always dress in dark indigo–coloured rags and on their heads they wear a turban of the same sombre colour, which they bring to a long point; and on this point they insert two or three of those iron hoops called quoits. These they use with wonderful dexterity and with little consideration. When these savages marched, or hopped and skipped, by, Runjeet increased his guard and he moreover told my father that he always had them placed between a large body of well-armed men, which was the case on this occasion. None of the troops did anything but march by, but all returned much pleased with the extraordinary exhibition.

Thursday 16th   This morning at daylight Runjeet had out all his regular troops for my father's inspection. They were 30,000 in number (foot soldiers) and extended for three miles about, three deep. They were very neatly drest in white trousers, scarlet jackets and scarlet silk turbans with a little gold cord twisted about them. Some of the officers were very funny figures indeed, half-French, half-Asiatic. His artillery was also out, about sixty pieces. These are not despicable, but very badly horsed. In the evening we went all over his palace at Lahore; but we walked about until nearly dead with heat and fatigue without the least reward for our trouble, so far as the palace was concerned. It was very ruinous. But we were allowed to see Runjeet's regalia, amongst which is the celebrated diamond armlet called the Coë Nore (this is spelt as pronounced) [Koh-i-Nur] which is valued at three millions and a half pounds sterling. I took it in my hand to say I had had it. It was altogether handsomer than I expected, for they cut their stones in so ugly a manner that I had expected it to look like the drop of a chandelier, and it did look prettier than that. I shall now bring this portion of journal to a conclusion, for I have swelled it to an enormous size and alas! your poor eyes! With kindest love to all friends, believe me, my dear Mrs Chaplin,

Yours very affectionately,

I. Fane.

XIV

From Lahore, commencing March 17th 1837.

Friday 17th   This morning at daylight the troops forming the escort went through some manoeuvres for Runjeet's amusement. They acquitted themselves much to my father's satisfaction and very much to the old man's; so much so that on his return home he remarked that he had been led to believe that the discipline of the British armies was nothing but boast; but having had this opportunity of judging for himself he energetically exclaimed, 'What *lies* they told me!' At half past three R. exhibited the rest of his contingent troops. We ladies did not attend this because we found there were not to be any of the Ackalees present, and we did not care for anything else. We made a party to cross the river, which runs close to our camp, to visit a tomb which is on the other side. We found that in the days of its splendour it must have been very beautiful, and exactly in the style of the buildings at Agra. *Now* it is in a sadly dilapidated state, for whenever Runjeet wants to touch up the interior of his palace in Lahore he deprives this tomb of its ornaments. Just as we were going to dinner Shere Sing 'just dropped in' to present to His Excellency the produce of his sport (a goose I believe), and being in our dinner tent he went to look at the table prepared for our repast. He was delighted with it, and has determined to send an order by Mr Holroyd to

Calcutta to procure for himself the same articles as he there saw.

Saturday 18th   This morning we began with a review of Runjeet's troops. Christine and I determined upon being present at this, so we mounted an elephant and set off. After his troops had done (and N.B., the wise ones say they cannot manoeuvre a bit and would have a very *very* poor chance fairly opposed to us), our artillery (black) did some practice for the old man's amusement. There were what are called, in military phraseology, curtains erected for the guns to point at and knock down. I am happy to tell you that this was beautifully done. You must understand it is right to take as much interest in black John Company soldiers as you do in white Europeans. I do my duty amply in this respect, for I think it much more interesting when they do well than when a white man does. After the curtains were well demolished Runjeet, I suppose attributing their demolition more to chance than skill, sent out to a certain distance from the guns a large and fine silk umbrella to be fired at. This was a most exciting moment, for if the gunners had failed how mortifying it would have been! But no such calamity befell us, for an early shot went through the umbrella, upon which occasion I gave such a shout of delight that some of the Seik soldiers, who were on horseback close by, burst into laughter at my ecstasy. The guns upset the umbrella over and over, and it was then brought in triumph to old Runjeet, who rewarded handsomely the officers and men.

Tonight Runjeet gave an entertainment for us ladies, and we saw him face to face for the first time. At a little after six we set off for the palace at Lahore. Upon my father's arrival in a certain enclosed space within the castle, a salute was fired, the guns being placed inside this square enclosure. Christine and I had squeezed into one palanquin, and we thought we were killed, for the smoke and fire wandered about so much that it seemed to come into the machine where we were, and right into our faces. At length we arrived safely at our destination and the moment we had so ardently wished for came, namely the one when we were to be introduced to Runjeet. We found him squatted on a chair with his legs tucked up, drest in the same dress I have before described. He had on no ornaments save two rows of very fine pearls round his wrist. His head was enveloped in a low kind of red gauze turban, which was neither pretty nor becoming. He is exceedingly ugly, but not unprepossessing-looking. The eye left him is prominent and bloodshot, and he does not seem to see over well with it. He was most gracious, and after we had been seated a few minutes he dismissed the greater number of his courtiers because he thought we would not like to be stared at by them. I sat next but one to him, so had my wicked will of staring at him. Because I was the great man's daughter he fed me with his own fingers, through the *hands* of another, with quail curry, which after pretending to taste I deposited into Captain Hay's glove, prepared for the purpose. The gentlemen drank the burning hot stuff I have mentioned before and the ladies were offered it; but on his being told it was not our custom to drink such strong drink, we were excused. We had nautching and fireworks and retired from *The Presence* at about nine o'clock. The apartment in which we sat was very curious and pretty. We were very hot, for although drest in evening gowns we were each compelled to put on a shawl, so as not to shew a bit of neck. On this occasion Runjeet gave my father a string of pearls and a fat horse richly caparisoned; and my father gave him a beautiful ivory and gold walking stick, which he had brought from England.

Sunday 19th There is an unfortunate English woman here, whose husband is in Runjeet's service. I don't know who he is or anything about him. They called upon us today. They march when R. marches and encamp when he encamps and are not stationary for long together. *She* would be to be pitied, only she chose her own fate. She is young, and would be pretty, but she has a very red face. She came all the way from England to marry this Mr Van Courtland,★ and I believe their acquaintance was formed at school. It is to be hoped they may not tire of each other. This afternoon Henry (my brother) and Mr Holroyd went by appointment to visit Runjeet. He wished to talk *law* with the latter. On their way there they were attacked by the fanatics I have mentioned, called Ackalees. One put something into their buggy which they both swear to have been a pistol, and on their return to camp they were again attacked by them. One aimed a blow at Mr Holroyd with a stick, which he parried with his whip, and so escaped unhurt. This adventure alarmed us much, for we were going with the rest of the ladies in camp by appointment to pay a visit to Runjeet's wives immediately on the return of the gentlemen. After due deliberation it was determined we might venture, by taking another route, with a strong Seik guard and the Political Agent.

We reached our destination perfectly safely. Runjeet had assembled his wives together in a tent in a flower garden. It appears they don't all put up together in one zanana, but were thus congregated for our accommodation. The tent was handsome, but small. We found him bundled up on a chair, surrounded on each side and behind with these his loves. There were ten of

★ He entered British employment on the outbreak of war with the Sikhs, and rendered valuable service as Commandant of the Hariana Light Horse during the Mutiny.

them, and each had a female attendant with a punkah, to drive away the flies. They all got up on our entrance, as well as the old man, who shook hands with us and introduced us to the mother of Khurrack, his eldest son; but about the others he said nothing. She was old, wizened, fat and hideous; indeed, with the exception of two or three they all were. These few exceptions were younger and prettier than one expected to find the property of an old decrepit man. They were all very handsomely drest, in gauzes with gold borders, and their arms, from wrist to elbow, covered with bracelets. Their ears, noses and foreheads were also much ornamented. They seemed in great awe, but very careful of their old man, for if a fly perched on him they directly took their chuddahs [*caddar* – shawl, mantle] to drive it off. Strange to say, he admitted into his harem on this occasion the minister's son, a youth of about sixteen, who is a great favourite, and his own grandson, the heir apparent. Us ladies he seated on chairs and made us draw in as close as we could. We thus formed a tight circle. Christine took her baby, and Mrs Torrens her boy and child of about five years old, and these two played together in the middle. The old boy is very fond of children, and he was delighted. He took our baby in his arms and paid him much attention. We took our maids with us, mine by way of an interpretess, Christine's for the child. We staid about twenty minutes and did not get on *very* well with our talk, for the language spoken here is very different from what my maid speaks; so each party had difficulty in understanding the other. Ere we took our departure we received magnificent presents, particularly Christine and I. Mine were the best, hers next. Mine consisted of a string of pearls with an ornament attached to it; a double row of pearls about the size of peas, but not particularly well-shaped or of good colour; an ornament for the head, value

210

about 300 rupees, which I think hideous; a pair of bracelets; a whole suit of native dress, which is curious and beautiful; and a gold parasol with a silver stick, the gold part composed of the same sort of stuff as that which Mrs Fane has sent to England for turbans. Whether I am allowed to keep these is a point to be settled. I have made up my mind I shall not. My father has made some representation to Lord Auckland on the subject. I believe he wants to be allowed to keep what he has received and pay himself all the expenses John Company will have incurred. I want to sell my ugly jewellery and buy with the money a handsome shawl.

Monday 20th   This morning at daylight my father accompanied Shere Sing on a shooting excursion. The first game they fell in with was a covey of *crows* sitting on the ground eating dirt. Shere fired at these and killed six, which he presented to my father. They then tried their skill in spearing the wild hog, and Shere put an end to one in this way in very good style. For beaters they had out a whole battalion of regular troops and they took besides a six-pounder cannon! The whole thing was so totally different from our idea of a chase that it was said to be very entertaining. In the afternoon my father went to visit Khurrack Sing in his tent. We had a large dinner party in the evening, and there were present Shere Sing and two other natives, who were magnificently drest. The former was not. These of course were mere spectators. They took no part in the proceedings. We had also all the Frenchmen, and most thankful I was when the party was over. It was a curious mixture of nations and languages, and this was the first time that any of these Seik grandees had been thus admitted into the private society of a European family.

Tuesday 21st The lancer part of the escort went out this morning to go through their lance exercise for Runjeet's amusement. In the afternoon Mr Holroyd and I went to see a faquir who has gained an immense reputation in consequence of having at various times shut himself up in a box which has been put into a hole in the earth and there allowed to remain for a certain time. He was said to be thus interred seven months upon the last occasion. This evening the French gents gave us a great dinner. They live about three miles from our camp and we had to go through the fort of Lahore, which looked very grand by the light of the bright moon. They had brilliant illuminations as you approached. They received us in a very beautiful tent and here we remained until dinner was announced. We dined in another large tent and this was the fun! Shere Sing was there, and several other of Runjeet's head people. These, as they don't take part in what is going on, sit behind the company. I wish I could give you an idea of a great dinner in India, but it is impossible for anyone who has not been present at one to conceive anything like their tediousness, or anything to be compared with their suffocation. This out-Heroded Herod, for besides our own attendants (who are so numerous as to entirely exclude the air), we had these natives and theirs, and besides these again, curiosity people, who completely stuffed up the doorways into the tent. So we had not a breath of air. When this charming repast was over we adjourned to the house, which was very curious and beautiful. We lent them our European band, and they had also a very tolerable one of their own. They wanted us very much to dance, which my father forbad our doing on account of the presence of the natives, for if we had they would have thought we did it for *their* amusement instead of our own, and our names would probably have been roughly handled in the newspapers. The French generals got into

212

trouble on the subject, for they had reckoned without their host and had promised these fellows we should dance. They were very angry and disappointed because we had not done so. I am delighted we did not, as we would have been made puppets for the amusement of the natives. We did not get away until late and I never was more sick of anything; indeed, I shall have a Frenchman fever if we don't leave this soon. If I spoke French well I should not mind them.

Wednesday 22nd The French General, Court, breakfasted with us. He is a philosopher, or rather savant. He brought to show my father a very curious collection of coins he has made in this country, as well as guns, antiques etc. He insisted upon Christine and I accepting what we looked upon as the most interesting things in his whole collection. We tried our utmost to resist, but to no purpose; so she is rich in the possession of a beautiful cameo found in Peshawur [Peshawar]. It is injured, but this adds to its curiosity. The subject is the marriage of Amphitrite and the carving is beautiful. Mine is a kind of cameo also; the subject a beautifully finished head of the Mogul Emperor, Shah Jehan.

Today commenced a holy festival known as the festival of the Hoolie [Holi]. It is the custom at this time for the Hindoos to bedaub each other with a red powder and other dirt. The Seiks are not Hindoos, but they also keep this festival; so Runjeet asked my father and staff to go to his residence and assist in the bedaubing. They all took the precaution of dressing in white clothes, and most fortunate it was they did so, for such objects as they returned eyes never saw. Sweeps in England on May Day they were *most* like, but I think even these are clean to them. They were a mass of red and yellow – skin, hair, clothes, all begrimed. They all fared alike, from King Runjeet to my father and all his staff. I have just learnt that this festival is a rejoicing for the coming of the spring (N.B. the thermometer yesterday at eleven o'clock was 86, and this is spring!). It also commemorates some improprieties that took place between their god, Krishna, and some young lady, so I am told a great many naughtinesses take place amongst the natives at this season. The Seiks are not quite Hindoos, but profess some of their tenets. They hate the Mussalman. This is an odious time, for the people make such a noise and get so drunk. One of Dr Wood's servants has died of intoxication and half of ours have been punished for disorderly conduct. It only lasts two days.

Thursday 23rd Baby very ill with dysentery. This complaint is very common to children teething in this country, and he is about cutting several teeth. It is said to do good instead of harm, provided it does not go on too long. Mr Holroyd drove me in a buggy this evening to see by daylight the Shalemar Gardens. They are about three miles from hence and are the gardens where Runjeet gave us the entertainment which I before mentioned. No native building bears a daylight inspection, and the one in the midst of this garden, which looked so well when illuminated, is not an exception to this general rule.

Friday 24th Good Friday. Alas! there is little to make one feel this day as one *ought* in the Punjaub and as one *would* in one's own country. In the afternoon I went on an elephant with Mr Holroyd through the city of Lahore. Every native city is dirty to a degree, but this beats all I have seen hollow. There were only two buildings therein (and these looked like mosques) that were handsome; all the rest of the houses were tumbledown, miserable places.

214

Saturday 25th   A very interesting event took place this afternoon, which I mounted my elephant to endeavour to see as much of as I could. A great Afghan chief, whom Runjeet has subdued, as good luck would have it, came today from his country for the purpose of presenting a celebrated horse, which the old gentleman had some years previously set his heart upon.* He had then given out that he never would see this chief's face in his own territories unless the horse accompanied him; which meant he never would render him any assistance when in need unless he obtained his wish. At this time they want Runjeet's patronage, and so this was the day on which the chief, Peer Mohomed Khan [Pir Muhammad Khan], was introduced and gave up the horse. My father was asked to be present, and cannot you fancy the gratification it must have been to old R. to have his piece of diplomacy *tell* in the presence of the Commander-in-Chief. He showed his gratification by strokes of his grey beard, these being as sure indications of his feelings as the rise or fall of the quicksilver is of the weather. After the Afghan chief had said his say he mounted his steed and marched past at the head of his troops. I was beautifully situated for seeing this, as they all passed within one yard of my elephant's head. I never saw so wild-looking a set of men. They seemed to dress as fancy dictated, and were *so* dirty. Some few had on chain armour, but they were all mounted on such sorry steeds. Their band was capital, and music divine! It is difficult to say whether *I* was more astonished at them, or *they* at seeing an unblushing, unveiled woman. It is not clear that they knew *what* I was – whether masculine

* This could refer to the famous mare, Laila, which belonged to the Governor of Peshawar, Yar Muhammad Khan. Ranjit claimed to have captured it, at the cost of much treasure and many men, in 1826; but Miss Fane's account appears to confirm, what has long been suspected, that another animal had been substituted for the coveted mare on the earlier occasion.

or feminine or neuter! After it was over I waited to see old Runjeet get into his glass palanquin, and this by the bye was the very last sight I had of him. When his one eye caught sight of me he sent to hope my health was good, and so departed. His prime minister mounted *the* horse and followed the palanquin. I also left, much delighted at my successful expedition.

Sunday 26th   Shocking to relate, at daylight there was a military spectacle of our cavalry and artillery for Runjeet, which I grieve to say I could not resist attending. They did their manoeuvres very well. After ours had finished Runjeet's infantry and artillery went through, for the first time, some manoeuvres which they had picked up from us since our residence at Lahore; and wonderfully well they were said to have done them. The general who commanded on the occasion was about sixteen years of age, and in consequence of his skill was presented with a village! Don't be astonished at this gift until you *see* the villages here. I spent such a wretched day and could do nothing I ought, for the French officers had given out that they were one and all coming some time between the hours of eleven and one to take leave of us. I had such a King Agrippa. At length they came, staid a very little while and went away. But there was one nice fat charmer who stopped for a minute behind the rest to crave a favour at our hands – and what do you think it was? Why, to be *allowed* the great gratification of giving Christine and me a shawl! It was the same dear fatty who gave us the antiquities, and he was then so hurt at our refusal to rob him that we *kindly* granted him this request; so in the afternoon there arrived for each of us two as handsome shawls as Lahore could furnish. John Company cannot touch these, so I am now the mistress of *three* magnificent ones, a black, a white and a blue. The latter

216

Henry gave me, another of the Frenchmen having given him two blue ones on a prior occasion. He gave me one, Christine the other. It turned out such a stormy evening, and thundered, lightened, hailed and blew tremendously, which we much rejoiced at, for it would lay the dust for our march and cool the air again for a few days. The baby still continues very ill. He had five teeth let through his gums with the lancet in the course of the day.

Monday 27th   Mr Vigne the traveller paid us a visit. He also gave Christine and me some pretty things which he had collected on his travels. He gave me a curious Caubul looking-glass frame, made of jasper, with some precious stones about it; also a very pretty jasper cup and saucer and a little antique for a ring; but he has given me what I prize more than all – *viz* a sketch he took of Runjeet, which is very like. At five o'clock my father, with a large retinue, went to bid adieu to our poor dear old entertainer. This was to have taken place on Sunday, but the astrologers pronounced Monday to be an unlucky day for the departure and Runjeet in consequence requested my father to remain until Tuesday. The interview took place in a tent in the midst of a garden, just without the city of Lahore. (He has never lived in the palace since we have been here and only went to it the night he entertained us, for that purpose.) He appeared, they told me, quite sorry to part, which feeling won't last long methinks, for we must have drained his coffers as well as his shawl repository and jewel ditto, the poor dear liberal old man! He gave many presents on this occasion. My father's were very handsome, consisting of shawls, kincobs, silks, satins, horses with their trappings, a beautiful sword, jewellery, etc., etc. To him and M. Beresford he gave a thing to tie round their necks which he called an order

217

or badge of honour, and one he desired to be given to Lord Auckland. So now I suppose they may call themselves Barons of the Punjaub! Henry's presents were also handsome, because he is the son of the great man; but all the other A.D.C.s fared very badly. They only got a pair of gold bangles each and a tunic-shaped embroidered dress, or rather coat. There was nothing else. Some were embroidered in gold, some in silver and others merely like the shawls. John is so disgusted with his he let me play a hit at backgammon for it. I have won it, so if John Company does not get it, it is mine.

Tuesday 28th   At five o'clock this morning we bad adieu to Lahore, and that with pleasure, for we had attained all our objects and for the last three days had had nothing to see; and as the heat was great, the flies very troublesome and the water so bad as to disarrange many stomachs, we had reasons to wish to depart. Our medical man, Dr Wood, is to be left for twenty days to try what he can do for Runjeet's paralysis. It is a fine thing for him, for whether he cures him or not he will make mints by trying his best. He will travel dak★ and reach Simla about the same time we do. On our way out of camp a salute was fired to our host. Shere Sing accompanies us as far as the Sutledge again. They went out shooting in the afternoon and killed two *doves* – and these by my father at Shere's request as they sat on a bush! What would the cocked-hat plantation say to this!

Thursday 30th   I forgot to mention it before, but during the whole of our stay at Lahore we had a dreadful case of smallpox in our camp. The young man

★ See Introduction, Section 4.

so afflicted was a first cousin of Mrs Thoby Prinsep's, a Mr Impey. He belonged to the 18th N[ative] I[nfantry], which has been our escort the whole of the march. It has been confluent, of the worst kind. The day before we left Lahore the poor young man's symptoms mended a little, and it was judged best he should proceed with the camp rather than be left behind, which it was at first thought must be done. But to end my story, this morning at ten o'clock he died. He was only nineteen years of age, was six feet five inches in height and, as all unnaturally tall men are, was as thin as a lath. He arrived in this country at the same time we did. No doubt his friends will set down his death to the climate; but if ever there was a judgement from heaven for a man's sins, I see it in his sickness and death. I cannot tell you the history of it, for it is not pretty. His dead body was brought on to this ground for interment, and our camp *wine chests* are to be made into a coffin for him. Every precaution has been taken to prevent contagion. His tent has been isolated, a guard put round it, and no soul but a European soldier to attend him allowed to approach him. At the same time I should not like to be one who *feared* the malady. H. Fane was vaccinated some weeks before the complaint made its appearance, so Mrs E. Fane need not be uneasy about her baby.

The name of the place we reached today is Kusoor [Kasur]. It belongs to Runjeet and gave him much trouble to subdue. It is famous for its manufacture of native saddles, and the people here embroider beautifully in gold on leather. In the afternoon I accompanied my father on horseback through the city. We found it much cleaner and altogether nicer than most native cities. My father bought a saddle, bridle and all the etceteras for a riding horse. The equipment was complete, with a good deal of gold embroidery about it, and fancy its costing the large sum of 28s English money! In my way through the town I spied out such a

219

pretty pair of silver earrings, which I tried hard to purchase; but they were prepared for a wedding which was just about to take place, and nothing would induce the old manufacturer to part with them. Before we had finished our ride we were joined by Shere Sing, which I mention to tell you an anecdote, in order to show you the estimation in which our sex is held in this country. My father pulled up to say how d'ye do to him, and as I did not want to do the same Captain Campbell and I rode on. We had two Seik soldiers before us, who were acting as guides, and the act of going in advance of the great men was so contrary to their notions of propriety that at length they observed that 'Memsahib (meaning me) ought not to be in advance of the Lord Sahibs' – meaning my father and Shere; to which Captain Campbell replied that 'in our country it was the custom for *ladies* to go before everyone' – a light which astonished them very much and made them laugh excessively. At sunset Mr Impey was buried on a high bit of ground at the end of the camp. The third round of firing over the grave took place just as we were riding into camp, and Shere requested permission to go and strew the grave with flowers, as a mark of respect. As soon as he had so done he sent for two shawls, which he spread over the grave and which he ordered to be left there until the grave was properly bricked up. He also placed two sentries over it, who were not to stir until this was done; and he has ordered a faquir to receive two rupees per month to watch and pray by the grave. The morning he heard of the young man's death he ordered no food to be cooked that day, which is what they practise themselves when in grief. All these were pretty attentions towards the nation, and showed good feeling in the individual. The poor young man was more honoured in his death than he ever was in his lifetime.

Friday 31st We encamped this morning on the banks of the Sutledge. In the afternoon there was a durbar for the purpose of bidding adieu to Shere Sing. On the occasion my father presented him with a very nice buggy, formerly the property of my brother, with a horse to draw it, and one of his own Europe guns. This was to have been the last we saw of him, but a report reached camp that three tigers were in the jungle on the other side of the river, so he was invited to cross and take part in the sport. This was done the following morning.

Saturday April 1st I crossed the Sutledge on an elephant with John. The animal stepped into a big boat. We did not dismount, but were safely ferried over in this way. John has got a bad boil on his leg and is obliged to march in the best manner he can. We had to march seven miles after crossing the Sutledge, and our howdah was so badly put on that we ran great risks of tumbling off; but after stopping twice to have it righted the last endeavour was crowned with success. At about eleven o'clock the sportsmen reached camp, without having seen the shadow of a tiger. Fortunately it was a nice cloudy day and some rain fell, so they were not roasted as well as disappointed. The baby is very ill today, so as to alarm the doctor, but alas! alas! the man who is acting during Dr Wood's absence is such a dreadful idiot that no one has the least confidence in him. Some of the officers who joined us to increase the escort to Lahore, and who are now going to leave, dined with my father. Christine and I cut them, because there was a difficulty about the tent accommodation, and we *teaed* with Marc, who continues confined to his couch. We are very uneasy about him, inasmuch as we think that his nerves have more to do with his illness than his body and that if he

221

would rouse himself it would be better for him. He has not taken part in any of the fun at Lahore.

Sunday 2nd   Today we halted. In the evening I rode out with my father, Captain Wade (the Political Agent) and H. Fane. The two last rode on horses which had been presented by the Maharajah. The one H. rides is my father's, and he likes it very much. The greater number presented in this way are of a very cart-horse style. Runjeet gave my father such a very curiously marked pony which, if it should live, he talks of carrying to England. It is marked just like a zebra, the black and white being beautifully clear and distinct. Mr Holroyd left us today at three o'clock on his return to Calcutta. He is to travel the whole distance, with the exception of about thirty miles, on men's shoulders, i.e. in a palanquin. He is about 1,400 miles from Calcutta and will be there by the 23rd, having stopped three days at Delhi, three at Agra and a day or so with the W. Fanes at Allahabad. Is it not a wonderful mode of conveyance?

Tuesday 4th   John drove me the march this morning in a buggy. His boils are very bad, so he chooses an easy mode of conveyance. He looks such an object, for he is starving and physicking for them. I have got a very sore finger, but fortunately *for you* it is one on my left hand. The baby was much better today. I rode out in the evening but saw nothing but corn fields. Just as we were about to go to tea Shere Sing came to our feeding tent. He chose to stay to see how and what my father ate, and then to see him play a rubber of whist. I wished him hanged, for my father sent a message to my tent to say I was not to come to our feeding tent until Shere was gone; and as my eyes just now are so

222

bad (because I have been such an idiot as to attempt to draw) I did not like the idea of spending the evening alone and unable to amuse myself. Why H.E. took this whim into his head I cannot imagine, because twice I have dined in Shere's presence and lots of times have been out riding with him. Fortunately H. Fane came to my rescue, so we took a small walk. Then he chaperoned me to Marc's tent and we sat with him until half-past eight o'clock, when I went to bed.

I have been actually compelled to make a pause in my journal from this date until now, the 19th. I chose, like a fool, to do two drawings, and by these means so completely ruined my eyes I have not been able to do an earthly thing but wind worsteds since. I should still, though, have continued this to you had there been anything the least worth putting on paper; but we have done nothing but march without seeing anything, so I took advantage of it to give my eyes a holiday. We encamped at the foot of the mountains yesterday, April 18th; the name of the place Bar. Here according to current account we were to have died of the heat; but this turned out, as all other reports *en route* have done, a fallacy. In excuse for those who unnecessarily alarmed us I must add that the season has been most favourable and cooler than usual, so that in our large tents, with the help of wetted cuscus [*khas* – vetiver], windows and punkahs, we have done very well, although the glass *in the shade* has stood at 96. At this place we have to bid adieu for a season to tents, carriages, horses, soldiers and, in consequence, to old friends, *viz* Captain Anson etc. In the evening Christine and I and the two H. Fanes mounted our ponies (which are to convey us up the mountains and to ride when at our homes at Simla) in order to practise our nerves for the ascent the following morning. We went for about a mile and a half and found it most fatiguing. We returned home to tea and a very early bed hour, *viz* a little after eight; and this we did because Christine and I and John were going to set off at two o'clock the following morning on our ascent up the Himalayas.

The moon is nearly full at this time, so it was very light when we started. The conveyance in which people go who do not ride is a thing which I can only compare to an open sedan chair. It is borne by four men, on their shoulders, and is rather a cramped conveyance for a journey of many miles. Some of the ascents and descents and sharp turns were so frightful that from sheer fright I actually cried. I had no spectator to my tears, which I just mention to prove how nervous I must have been, and how frightful the road, for I am not in general the least of a coward. It was moonlight when we started, but for about half an hour before sunrise it was dark, and we had torches – which was the greatest relief to me, as by this light I could not see the precipices. We reached our first halting place, *viz* Sabatoo [Subathu] at seven o'clock in the morning. An officer of a rifle corps which is quartered here (composed of Gourkas) vacated his house for us, and here we halted Wednesday and Thursday. We dined with the Colonel on Wednesday, and on Thursday some military manoeuvres took place. Sabatoo has a most curious appearance. You come upon it suddenly after scrambling up and down mountains. It is a bit of green table land, and the bungalows are prettily scattered about. The wind whilst we were here was very high, and we were very cold. This was the first time my father and I had slept in a house since we had left Allahabad in the month of November. We ate here excellent strawberries, the product of Colonel Tapp's garden.

The next morning John and I started in company for our next halting place, a dak bungalow at a place called Syree. This we reached by about seven o'clock.

We here washed and dressed, breakfasted and had a cold dinner at two o'clock, after which we again set off for our mountain homes, which we reached by about six o'clock. The last nine miles of our journey were a most precipitous ascent, and the road wound in such a manner that we could see the point we had to gain, which appeared quite impracticable. However, we reached it, and that without accident; but Oh Heavens! the narrowness of the road, and the precipices! My brother is so nervous on these occasions he has walked pretty nearly half the way, and has made his feet very bad by it. My father rode hill ponies, excepting when a descent was very steep, and then he got into his jonpaun [*janpan* – sedan chair for hilly districts]. The scenery the whole of the way, with the exception of the last five miles into Simla, is very grand, awful, terrific, but not in the least pretty from the almost total absence of trees and verdure. The above-named five miles are very pretty, or rather very beautiful, for the mountains are a mass of the scarlet rhododendron, which here grows as a tree, and not as a shrub as we have it in England. The bungalows are beautifully situated upon the sides of the different mountains, and altogether Simla has a very striking appearance. Our house is 7,800 feet above the level of the sea, and the thermometer in the shade at noon stands at 65. At Bar we had it at 96 in the shade. The house, which used to be Lord William Bentinck's, we found a very good one. We have an excellent dining and drawing room, and an enclosed verandah, which we put furniture in. It makes a third nice room. The bedrooms would be good, only they are so dark, which is a drawback to their comfort. Henry and Cos are the only individuals housed here besides my father and self, and our maids. Edward has a snug small house to himself, the property of my father and therefore rent-free, and is delighted with it.

225

John has another, which he rents, and which he is charmed with also. It has a piece of ground attached to it, which he intends to cultivate. Captain Hay has another, and Marc and Captain Campbell and Dr Wood occupy a house amongst them. Poor Marc is in despair about his – as well he may be, for his share of it is the picture of dirt, desolation and misery; and as he is still an invalid and confined to his couch, and his spirits are very downcast from his long confinement, his discomfort is a great misfortune. The whole of the house is equally bad, but messrs. Wood and Campbell, having no office, can contrive to make their dog-hole look neater. At half-past seven, when we sit down to dinner, we have our window curtains let down and a fire besides – and this in India!

We have since our arrival here received late English news per newspapers, but I am sorry to say not by letter. The influenza seems to have made sad havoc, and I fear to it may be attributed the death of Mr James Praed, which I read of with the sincerest regret. God grant all friends in Lincolnshire have escaped and are well. I had a letter yesterday from Miss Eden, who tells me Lady Caroline Hatton is going to marry Mr Turner, and Lord Winchelsea Miss Bagot. The former did not surprise me, the latter did. We are all well. John is still *biley*, i.e., has got boils. And now, dear Mrs Chaplin, adieu. We send our very best love, and particularly I send mine to your dear kind mother. Ever believe me

Yours very affectionately,

I. Fane

Simla, April 24th 1837

226

THE JOURNAL OF ISABELLA FANE

THE JOURNAL OF ISABELLA FANE

The foregoing is the last of the surviving letters of Isabella Fane, but in her journal we have a regular if less detailed account of her remaining period in India. Not that there was much to record in Simla. The tiny station of those days was the despair of diarists and correspondents. Its fund of interesting topics was soon exhausted, because one lived there remote from native life, meeting the same people day after day and mechanically following the spa-like sequence of morning visits, afternoon airings and evening dinner parties and card games. Henry Edward Fane decided that there was no point in continuing his diary. 'The sameness of our lives here', he wrote, 'unless I make an expedition into the interior, will not make it worthwhile to continue my journal until we again descend into the plains. I shall therefore shut the book until that event occurs.' Isabella carried on with her journal, though its brief entries reflect little save the monotony of her existence. Even momentous news lost its impact in that rarefied atmosphere. On September 8th, 1837, Simla heard that it had entered the Victorian age; but the intelligence was hardly blazed forth by the heavens themselves. 'Decided accounts reached us today of the death of His Majesty King William the 4th', noted Isabella laconically, adding: 'Captain Bean came to tune the piano.' The blossoming courtship of Marc Beresford and Caroline Fane was more disturbing; it threatened both family harmony and personal equanimity. 'Went out in my jonpaun with Marc', she noted on July 20th, 'and was much fussed by information he gave me.'

The highlight of the summer was an expedition to Kotgarh, an alpine retreat in the foothills beyond Simla. Isabella passed a happy fortnight in the company of Henry Edward Fane and Captain Campbell, exclaiming at the magnificent scenery, picknicking under horse-chestnut trees, collecting botanical specimens and enjoying the half-forgotten luxuries of mulled claret and blazing fires. On June 2nd they ascended Hatu peak, 10,000 feet above sea level, where 'there was much snow immediately around us, and we used solid blocks of it to cool all the things we took up to drink for luncheon.'

With the onset of the cold weather in October, Sir Henry Fane and his entourage descended from the hills and set off again on a tour of inspection, this time of British garrisons in the Delhi Territory. For two months life was once more all nerve-racking bustle and dusty confusion, interlarded with durbars and parades. On November 3rd, at a reception given by the Patiala Raja, Isabella's elephant bolted, frightened by a firework, and 'tore with us through flower beds, hedges, ditches, etc., etc.' But she lived to tell the tale. 'Fortunately, after going his best pace for about a mile he became fatigued and stopped of his own accord. We had a most fortunate escape with our lives, and were well satisfied that the result was merely much tearing of gowns, collars, etc.'

The visit to Hansi, in November, was enlived by the presence of the legendary James Skinner, a Eurasian adventurer with many colourful tales to tell of service with the native princes in the old days. His remarkable services under the British flag had enabled him to surmount both official and unofficial prejudice against people of mixed parentage and he carried the King's brevet rank of Lieutenant-Colonel and the decoration of Companionship of the Bath. His corps of irregular horse were famed for their bravery and skill, but Isabella found that their feats did not live up to expectations. 'We were all much disappointed, as at Astley's we had seen much better.' (Astley's was a well known London theatre, specializing in circus entertainment.) More intriguing was a visit to Skinner's wife and daughter-in-law. 'They are natives and live behind the purdah', she noted, 'but they have many privileges above those which their sex usually enjoy in this country, as they see not only the female, but also the male friends of their husbands.' Both were covered with jewels, and the younger *bibi* was very fair, 'as fair as a European', though not such a beauty as her reputation had suggested. The climax of the tour was a halt in Delhi, the old Mughal capital, from November 30th until December 11th. Isabella found the city very fine, and was particularly impressed by the Jama Masjid ('Friday Mosque') – 'a very magnificent building, and in beautiful preservation' – though the eagerly anticipated multitude of the faithful failed to materialize at prayer-time on Friday. The feelings aroused by a visit to the Red Fort, residence of the Emperor, were those of melancholy. 'It is all in the most ruinous state, and all his dependents look so shabby and poor. Even the prime minister looks like a chimney sweep.' The Great Mughal himself she did not see, since she was compelled by the usual exasperating etiquette to remain invisible while her father paid his official respects. The loveliest thing that Delhi had to show was the Qutb Minar, an early Islamic victory tower on the outskirts of the city. Isabella climbed to the top, but found the dreary view small compensation for the effort.

The Fanes returned to Simla *via* Alipur, Panipat, Karnal and Ambala, accompanied part of the way by Lord and Lady Cardigan, who had joined them at

Delhi. On December 21st, at Karnal, she got wind of the event she had long been expecting and dreading – the betrothal of Marc and Caroline. This seemed like a betrayal, and made her feel 'queer'. Her father heard of it a couple of days later, and was shocked and upset. 'It made me very unhappy', she wrote, 'to think that one I loved had acted, in my opinion, so badly . . . I went to bed very tired and sick at heart.' The news robbed Christmas of all its joy. 'We all agreed we were so depressed from the circumstances which had occurred that it was folly to pass the compliments of the day to one another.'

They arrived back in Simla early in January 1838, when the resort was almost deserted. 'We remained quietly shut up for the two following months', wrote Henry Edward Fane, 'thoroughly enjoying the bracing air and deliciously cold climate of the hills.' For Isabella it was a gloomy time. We can only guess about her feelings for Marc Beresford and John Michel, but it is hardly open to doubt that their weddings – Beresford's with Caroline Fane in January and Michel's with Louisa Churchill in May – made her feel lonely and ageing. With the loss of these two unattached male friends her own chances of marriage had almost vanished, for at thirty-four she was well past an eligible age. Beresford's second marriage was regarded as something of a scandal. 'He is here now with a second wife twenty years younger than himself', wrote Emily Eden from Simla in April, 'to whom he engaged himself three months after the first wife's death. Never told anybody, so we all took the trouble of going on pitying him with the very best pity we had to spare. Such a waste!' The quarrel between Isabella and the newly-weds was eventually patched up – partly through the good offices of Emily Eden – but she remained estranged from Caroline's parents, the Fanes of Allahabad. On January 21st she noted the arrival of a letter from Mrs William

Fane 'which was to decide that war was to be between us for the rest of our days'; and the rift was apparently still unhealed at the end of the year, because she makes no mention of visiting her aunt and uncle at Allahabad during her return journey to Calcutta. John Michel's wedding she took in better spirit, improvising an altar with clothes horses and shawls and officiating with Miss Bacon as bridesmaid. 'The bride looked lovely, in white satin with a veil and orange flowers intermingled in her hair.' The Governor-General and his suite attended the ceremony, and afterwards they all sat down to a huge dinner.

The arrival of Lord Auckland's party early in April brought the pleasure of reunion with the Misses Eden and ensured that Simla was more than usually gay that season. The Governor-General gave a grand ball in honour of Queen Victoria's birthday on May 24th – an occasion marred only by the bad weather, which put out half the illuminations; and throughout the summer there were picnics, garden parties and fancy fairs, all with unlimited strawberries and ice-cream. In June Isabella made an excursion to Chur Mountain, a landmark in the Himalayan foothills, in the company of Miss Bacon, Henry Edward Fane and Captain and Mrs Ponsonby. The stupendous alpine scenery put her in mind 'of the beginning of the world, or chaos'. The ascent of Chur Moutain, over 12,000 feet above sea level, was 'the most terrific thing I ever did, or hope I ever shall do . . . I had a rope tied round my waist, and a man pushed me from behind.' But nothing, alas, was to be seen from the summit. The eagerly anticipated view was obscured by mist. 'All we have left is to boast that we have accomplished what I feel convinced few ladies have done or ever will do.' They returned to Simla minus Miss Bacon, who left them to go on to Mussoorie. 'Henry in a sad state', noted Isabella a trifle waspishly, 'for he fancied himself desperately in love with her.'

Back in Simla, life's usual calm was ruffled. First there were the alarming antics of Major Slade, a member of her father's entourage, who became one of the unheroic and largely unrecorded casualties of the burden of empire. At the end of July he began to show symptoms of mental collapse, making himself, as Isabella noted, 'so odious, and so rude to me and so officious to the guests, that we pronounced him either mad or drunk.' On July 31st he was 'very outrageous . . . [and] twice came into the drawing room, whilst I was there, in only his shirt . . . He unsettled us completely and we did nothing but sit and talk about the pleasure of having a maniac in one's house.' A couple of days later 'three times he made his appearance at the drawing-room door, in which room I was sitting, with nothing on him but his shirt'; and at night he kept 'jumping in and out of bed, talking and laughing and writing charges against Dr Wood . . . and my father.' Opiates were given and leeeches applied; but all to no avail. He was finally carried away, raving, under a guard of Gurkhas – a rare reminder of the psychological stresses of service in India. From this time, too, the official comings and goings resulting from the Governor-General's presence began to acquire unwelcome significance, as portents of political crisis. As the summer advanced, the prospect of war grew to a certainty, and on August 21st Isabella recorded that she was made 'very unhappy by learning that my father's fate was sealed and that he must at least proceed to the neighbourhood of the seat of war, as far as he could, until the arrival of his successor.' It was now clear that her own oriental adventures were nearing their end, and that she and her sister-in-law, Christine, must return to England and leave their menfolk to the serious business of the fighting in Afghanistan. Many were the happy parties, like the Fanes', that broke up that autumn, never to be reunited.

234

The Fane women and children left Simla for good on November 3rd, and Isabella's journal ends on a forlorn note, with an account of her return journey towards Calcutta. This voyage was very different from the grand progress of two years before. She was no longer the Commander-in-Chief's hostess; only an unattached female who had become an encumbrance. She and Christine were in the charge of Raleigh Yea, who had succeeded Captain Campbell as Sir Henry Fane's A.D.C. in March, and who let it be known that he reckoned going with the women to be a poor substitute for going to the wars. His ungracious and querulous behaviour made a painful contrast to the chivalry of her male travelling companions of 1836. There were now no official receptions, and hardly a nod from the ladies in the up-country stations who had clamoured for an introduction when she passed their way before. 'We left Meerut somewhat disgusted with the Meerut folks', Isabella noted on November 26th. 'We set them all down for toadies, as they only notice us when we are with the great.' On November 28th they embarked to complete their voyage by river transport; but this time there was no official steamboat – only humble country budgerows. Isabella found her vessel 'much more spacious and convenient than I had anticipated', and soon had herself smugly installed with her cat and her piano; but it was not long before she began to be bothered by cockroaches, her old enemies the mosquitos, and the evil-smelling detritus of the Ganges. 'Saw such a dead Hindoo', she noted on December 20th, 'who nearly caught in Christine's boat.' Small wonder that we read of her taking castor oil for 'indigestion', and of her sending for Dr Beattie at Allahabad because she felt 'sick'. Confronting her tribulations with characteristic phlegm, Isabella turned to spinsterish consolations; and so, the sail of her budgerow swelling before the wind, she passes out of view, fussing over her cat, tinkling on her piano, and writing down her experiences for the beguilement of unknown posterity.

POSTSCRIPT

With her return from India Isabella's salad days were ended. She led the rootless existence of an unattached spinster of slender means and advancing years. Various members of the family offered her hospitality, but she felt that she belonged nowhere. After the death of her father the Fulbeck estate was taken over by her brother Henry and his wife Christine, with whom she found it increasingly difficult to live harmoniously. An additional surviving volume of her journal covers the period 1852–54, during which she was living abroad; initially at Boulogne and subsequently, after an intervening return visit to England, at Aix-la-Chapelle. It reveals a mundane existence, in which the only diversions were quarrels with landladies and the tantrums of a temperamental maid. 'I must bear with dulness', she wrote, 'since neither health nor purse will enable me to live in England.' She died in 1886, still unmarried, at Pau in southern France, where she is buried. One volume of her papers at Lincoln bears the inscription 'To be destroyed after my death'. Her instructions have been carried out, for the pages of the book are missing, and whatever secrets it contained have gone with our heroine to her grave.

INDEX

239

244

that I completely forgot about what to do with my face. And suddenly there I was, right in front of Mrs. Hata.

She was wearing a pair of baggy pants and one of Mr. Hata's old shirts, and she had a wide straw hat tied on her head to keep the sun off her face. She also had a hot water bottle tied on her back with a long piece of cloth. I guess her back was aching from all that work she had to do in the fields.

"Hello, Rinko," she said. "How nice to see you."

'I put out my hand, all solemn and serious, but instead of shaking it the way I expected her to, Mrs. Hata stuck a cucumber in it.

"Here," she said, "You can have that one."

I was so surprised, I burst out laughing. And Mrs. Hata laughed with me.

I was surprised she'd be so cheerful when she had so much to be miserable about. After all, her husband had just died, and she had to be out picking cucumbers on a Sunday afternoon with an aching back.

But that was only the first surprise. The second big surprise of the day came after we got home.